"The more you know about where you're going, the closer you are to being there..."

HIP POCKET GUIDE

TO PLANNING & EVALUATION

Dorothy P. Craig

The **Hip Pocket Guide** was developed and tested through the Community Mental Health Skills Laboratory, a project of the University of Michigan School of Social Work's Program for Continuing Education in the Human Services. The Lab was funded in part through a grant from the Continuing Education Board of the National Institute of Mental Health and was cosponsored by the Detroit–Wayne County Community Mental Health Board. Other training materials are available from the Program for Continuing Education in the Human Services, University of Michigan, School of Social Work, 1015 E. Huron, Ann Arbor, Michigan, 48109.

Library of Congress Cataloging in Publication Data

Craig, Dorothy P
  Hip pocket guide to planning and evaluation.

  Bibliography: p.
  1. Corporate planning. 2. Organizational effectiveness. I. Title.
HD3028.C7   658.4'01   77-13388
ISBN 0-89384-024-6

Learning Concepts

Distributed by University Associates, Inc.
8517 Production Avenue, San Diego, CA 92121

Edited by Linda Schexnaydre

Cover Design by Jimmy Hill
Book design and artwork by Suzanne Pustejovsky
Composition by Mary Ann Noretto

HIP POCKET GUIDE

CONTENTS

ACKNOWLEDGMENTS

This book was written one sunny spring when I had occasion to write down what I knew about planning and evaluation for use in a series of training sessions. The resulting **Hip Pocket Guide** is a collection of many people's ideas; these are acknowledged throughout the text. The book could not have been written, however, without certain people and the experiences I have shared with them.

Working with Bob Trenz, I learned that a Don Quixote lurks within nearly every bureaucrat and discovered the harmonious system of interrelationships behind the frustrating tangle of bureaucratic organization. At the same time, whenever I got carried away with such flights of fancy, Norm Hill was always there to remind me of the reality of organizational life and to challenge me to deal with it.

I am grateful to Marilyn Harris, Chuck Strawn, and Sherry McRill for showing me what a powerful learning experience a well-designed workshop can be, and to Lynn Deniston for providing a planning/evaluation model that not only is simple and coherent but actually works.

Finally, this book could not have been written without the help of my colleagues at the Mental Health Skills Lab—Celeste Sturdevant, George Mink, Jan Stark, and Chris Stillwell. As the book evolved from a short handout to a 90–page monster, they sweated with me through six weeks of training deadlines—brainstorming, critiquing, coaching, and finally co-training a group of Detroit community mental health program staff.

Dorothy P. Craig
Seattle, Washington
May, 1978

how to use
HIP POCKET

This guide to planning and evaluation was prepared for managers and professional staff in educational and human service organizations, government agencies, and private corporations. These organizations vary widely in size, purpose, and technology; but the skills and techniques used in planning and evaluation can be applied to nearly any problem in just about any organization. The basic concept behind this guide is that planning is a way of ordering the apparent uncertainty around us and of coping with demands that sometimes seem overwhelming. Evaluation is a way of staying on course and providing feedback to ourselves to make sure we are spending our time on the most important tasks. As we learn to set objectives, plan strategies, and obtain feedback, we can help our organizations operate more effectively, do our jobs better, and feel a greater sense of accomplishment for our efforts. Planning can and should be a tool for helping people take control of their lives and become more effective both personally and as a part of an organization.

In case you are wondering why this is called a "hip pocket guide," when it is much too big for most people's hip pockets, it is to emphasize that we are talking about a process that is USABLE. We are offering a set of techniques that you'll have readily at hand for solving immediate, day-to-day problems, as well as for developing short- or long-range plans. You can use **Hip Pocket Guide** in writing a grant application for outside funding or to justify a budget increase to your board of directors or your local government. You can use **Hip Pocket Guide** in your organization's planning sessions or to help manage your own job tasks.

The book presents some basic concepts about planning in a step-by-step way: defining problems, setting objectives, choosing among alternate strategies, preparing for implementation, designing evaluation, and using evaluative information. In reality, these steps do not occur in a simple linear fashion. Planning is a continual process of asking and re-asking questions: redefining the problem, restating the objective, thinking of new alternatives, remembering new resources or obstacles, asking new evaluative questions, using new sources of information.

This guide is not meant to be an exhaustive or in-depth treatment of the planning process. Rather, it has been developed as a basic primer, designed in workbook format, with space for you to work through your plan at each step of the way. You will find a case example provided throughout the book and sample worksheets completed for this example. The example involves the experiences of a hypothetical personnel manager of a city water department having several hundred employees. The personnel manager is a middle-aged, white male. His problem is

GUIDE

how to plan a process for recruiting and promoting minority and female employees. This problem was chosen because it is one faced by a variety of public agencies, nonprofit organizations, and private corporations. The problem-solving strategy that this example illustrates has an even broader application to a whole range of organizational problems. And the overall planning approach is applicable to just about any problem, ranging from prevention of unwanted pregnancies to homes needing repair to increasing production on the assembly line.

It should be emphasized that the conceptual exercises suggested here may be easy for some, difficult for others. No one planning technique works for everyone. You are encouraged to try these to see if they are right for you. When you've finished the **Hip Pocket Guide**, you'll be familiar with a variety of planning and evaluation tools. You'll be able to choose among them as new situations arise, and you'll probably be able to think of new techniques that will meet your own needs.

Before you begin using this workbook to develop your plan, read **Hip Pocket Guide** all the way through the Epilogue. You can use the planning steps on the next page to get an overview of the process you'll be following. Next, work through Parts A and B of the Epilogue. These steps will help you begin thinking about your attitudes toward change and your organization's likely response to change. These exercises are important because they will prepare you for the change that may result from your plan. You will find, as you develop your plan, that planning involves change and change is often difficult for people and for organizations. As you work through **Hip Pocket Guide**, remember that the most important thing is to think clearly through each step. Complete all the planning and evaluation steps in this manual *before* you start implementing your plan, and involve others from your organization as you do this.

Planning and evaluation are by nature orderly, analytical processes, the logic of which sometimes runs counter to the immediacy of day-to-day organizational life. Merely attempting to do planning and evaluation may require an organization to change some of its most time-honored traditions and practices. But it is becoming increasingly clear that organizations and individuals must change merely to cope with the many demands made on them. Planning and evaluation approaches such as the one described here will do more than merely help organizations cope with problems confronting them. In the long run, organizations which incorporate planning philosophies and techniques into their institutional lives will do a better job of accomplishing their organizational purpose and at the same time will provide a more rewarding environment for organizational members.

PLANNING STEPS

1 Defining the Problem

2 Setting the Objective

3 Choosing among Alternate Strategies

4 Preparing for Implementation

5 Designing the Evaluation

6 Using Evaluative Information

EPILOGUE Initiating Organizational Change

PLANNING QUESTIONS ?

What is the present situation?
Who says it's a problem?
What will happen if nothing is done?

What do I want the situation to be in the future?
How will I know when I have achieved it?

What are all the possible ways to solve the problem?
What resources would be needed to do each alternative?
Which alternatives are most feasible?
Who needs to be involved in choosing which way is best?

What arrangements need to be made with other organizations and
     people to carry out the plan?
How will we get everything done on schedule?
How will the needed resources be found?

How will I know when I've reached my objectives?
How well did the strategies and activities work out?
How efficiently were the resources used?

What will I do with this information?
Who needs to receive it?
How can I make it possible for others to use this information?

What is the organization's capacity for change?
How do organizations change?
What problems will I face in introducing my plan?
How can I get my plan accepted?

DEFINING THE PROBLEM
STEP 1

The first step in planning and evaluation is the one that is the most crucial, the most difficult, and the most often neglected. If this step is overlooked or done carelessly, the rest of the process may end up being completely off base; and we won't even know it until much later, after a lot of time, energy, and money has been wasted.

Too often planners assume that a "problem" is the "lack of a plan." For example, "The problem is that we don't have enough counseling services," or "We don't have enough training for our sales force." If these problem statements are not examined, they would be short, logical, but possibly wrong steps to designing a master plan for dozens of counseling centers or providing an expensive training course for the sales force. They lock us into one solution when there may be easier, cheaper, and better solutions to the real problems—that students are having personal and family crises that they are unable to deal with alone or that sales personnel have not reached targeted sales projections.

In the next few pages, you will work through these nine steps leading up to a formal statement of the problem.

A Start with a rough narrative description of the problem situation, and underline the key words.

B Write a more concise (one paragraph) statement of the problem.

C Figure out whose problem this is.

D Ask yourself what would happen if nothing is done about this problem.

E Consider whether it's appropriate for your organization to be doing something about this problem.

F Stop to be sure you can accept this problem as important and meaningful to you.

G Analyze the causes of the problem.

H Rewrite the problem statement based on your more complete understanding of the problem.

FINALLY...
Refine the problem statement.

The steps suggested here for defining the problem are intended to help you identify clearly the basic, underlying problem that you are trying to solve—not merely a solution masquerading as a problem. There are many definitions of what a "problem" is. This is the one we will use:

A PROBLEM is...

1. A situation or condition
2. of people or the organization
3. that will exist in the future and
4. that is considered undesirable
5. by the members of the organization.

The most important part of this definition is to think of the problem as something that will happen in the *future* if something isn't done. This "something" may be a *bad* consequence, such as students who drop out of school or get into trouble with the police, or a drop in sales, or high turnover of clerical staff. It may be a consequence that is just *not as good* as we would like; for example, students we know are troubled may continue not to seek help from school staff or secretaries with an interest in improving their skills may not have access to training opportunities.

Stating the problem in terms of a *future* situation will help you state the objective in Step 2 in a way that can be easily visualized and evaluated.

Start with a rough narrative description of the problem situation, and underline the key words.

Sample
Narrative Description of Problem—First Draft

Problem for the personnel manager of a city water department, as he first roughly describes it

Our department serves a medium-sized midwestern city having a minority population of about 20%. We have 400 employees, of whom 100 are technicians, 200 are laborers (mostly male), 50 are clerical (mostly female), 30 are supervisors (mostly male), and 2 are managers (the director and his assistant).

The mayor has just handed down a directive that all departments must have a <u>new Affirmative Action Plan</u> showing how we're going to <u>increase the number of minority and female employees</u> throughout the organization. It must be written and ready for implementation in six months, by the end of the fiscal year.

The mayor has just returned from a national conference where he heard about how another city is involved in an expensive civil rights <u>lawsuit</u> over the lack of a plan.

Meanwhile, a local <u>Chicano organization</u> has been picketing city hall, <u>complaining</u> that Chicanos can only get unskilled labor jobs. They claim that our <u>promotion practices are discriminatory</u>. The <u>newspaper</u> just did a story in conjunction with a women's rights conference in the city, emphasizing that city government has <u>very few women</u> in skilled jobs and management positions.

In our department there's a lot of <u>resistance</u> to changing the status quo.

The unions see this as a threat. But management wants to open up jobs to <u>new, untapped talent</u>.

Narrative Description of Problem—First Draft

This page is left blank so you can write a rough description of your problem situation. Try pretending you are writing a letter to a friend in another city and you want to explain all the key points.

STEP 1
B

Write a more concise (one paragraph) statement of the problem.

Sample
Concise Problem
Statement

The department is facing a federal government mandate to increase the numbers of minority and female employees. Local minority and women's groups are also exerting pressure on the department. A new Affirmative Action Plan must be ready for implementation in six months.

Concise Problem Statement

In the space below, try rewriting your problem in a brief paragraph.

Sample
Who experiences this as a problem?

The politicians, who are getting flack from newspapers, citizen groups, federal officials

My boss, who has to come up with a plan within six months

Me, who has to do the plan in six months

Minorities and women, who can't get jobs in the department

Minority and women's groups, who are exerting pressure for equal employment opportunity

Potential employees (white males), who'll be threatened by job competition

Present employees (white males), who'll resent giving a break to minorities and women

Present supervisors, who are afraid we'll hire people who can't perform

Who experiences this as a problem?

In the space below, identify who is affected by your problem.

STEP 1
D

Ask yourself what would happen if nothing is done about this problem.

Sample
What may happen if nothing is done?

The boss will be in trouble with the mayor.

I'll be in trouble with my boss.

Maybe nothing will happen, and the whole thing will blow over.

Somebody could file a discrimination suit against the city.

Some minority group could file a class action suit.

The department might lose out on some juicy federal grants.

For sure, we'll be hassled by the federal government.

The department will continue to hire mostly white males, except for clerical and unskilled labor jobs.

Maybe some good people won't come to work here.

What may happen if nothing is done?

In the space below, write down what might happen if nothing is done about your problem.

STEP 1

E

Sample Organization's Purpose

1. **What is the purpose of the organization?**
   The purpose of the city water department is to design, construct, and maintain the city's waterworks and ensure an adequate supply of water exceeding minimum health and fire safety standards.

2. **Does the problem "fit" the purpose?**
   Yes ( )   No ( )   Unclear (x)

3. **How is the problem related to the organization's purpose?**
   To fulfill its purpose, the department needs quality personnel and good employee morale. And the reality is that to receive federal funds, we need to comply with Affirmative Action Policy.

Organization's Purpose

In the space below, answer these questions about your organization and your problem:

1. **What is the purpose of your organization?**

2. **Does the problem "fit" the purpose?**
   Yes ( )   No ( )   Unclear ( )

3. **How is the problem related to the organization's purpose?**

STEP 1
F

Stop to be sure you can accept this problem as important and meaningful to you. If not, you are not likely to devote the time and energy that will be needed to solve it.

Sample
What's in it for me?

A paycheck. I get paid for doing what I'm told to do.

Satisfaction of helping the department stay out of trouble with the federal government and citizen groups.

If the mayor finds out I did a good job, he might nod at me in the hall sometime.

Gripes from some employees who'll think I'm trying to do them in.

If I handle this right, I might have a better chance at the assistant director's job when it opens up.

I believe everybody should have a fair chance to get a job or a promotion.

I believe minorities and women haven't had a fair chance in employment in the past, and I would like to do something to contribute to equal employment opportunity.

Is this problem important to me personally?
    Yes (x)   Sort of ( )   Not really ( )

What's in it for me?

In the space below, write down some "what's-in-it-for-me" statements about your problem.

Is this problem important to me personally?

Yes ( )   Sort of ( )   Not really ( )

Sample
What has happened to make this a problem?

The civil rights movement and riots of the 1950's and 1960's and the feminist movement of the 1970's made people in government decide to do something to force employers to hire and promote minorities and women.

Employers haven't hired minorities and women in the past because—

- They thought minorities and women didn't have the education or skills to do the job.

- They wanted to avoid racial friction among employees.

- They were prejudiced.

- They didn't think minorities or women wanted the jobs or promotions. (Nobody applied.)

- They didn't believe minorities or women could learn to do the job.

- They thought certain jobs should be done only by white males.

- They thought minorities and women should stick to their places.

- They didn't know minority people to refer for job openings.

What has happened to cause your problem?

In the space below, write down some things that have led to your problem situation.

H

Rewrite the problem statement based on your more complete understanding of the problem.

Sample Rewritten Problem Statement

In the past five steps, we have S-T-R-E-T-C-H-E-D our understanding of the problem by looking at it from a number of directions. Now it's time to distill the essence of the problem so that it is crystal clear. After thinking long and hard about the problem and doing some personal soul searching, our personnel manager rewrote his problem as shown below:

> The department does not have a process for hiring and promoting minorities and women that has the support of existing employees and supervisors as well as outside citizens' groups.

Rewritten
Problem Statement

In the space below, rewrite your problem in one concise sentence.

Sample
Final Problem Statement

The following five basic elements should be contained in the problem statement:

1. Future point in time that you're concerned about

2. Geographic area or parts of the organization that the problem affects

3. Nature of the problem

4. Estimate of the size of the problem

5. Individuals or groups of people the problem affects.

This is how the personnel manager refined his final problem statement.

> 1. **If something isn't done, six months from now**
>
> 2. **the city water department**
>
> 3. **will still not have a process for recruiting and promoting minorities and women**
>
> 4. & 5. **that has the support of all three employee unions, management, and six major community minority/women's advocate groups.**

Final Problem Statement

In the space below, rewrite your problem statement including the five basic elements. The hardest part will probably be estimating the size or extent of the problem. It's necessary to do this, however, so that you will have a way to measure how effective you've been in reducing the problem through your plan.

1.

2.

3.

4.

5.

SETTING THE OBJECTIVE

STEP 2

One of the most confusing things about objectives is figuring out the difference between "purposes," "goals," and "objectives." We all have our own definitions for these terms, so let's ignore this problem as much as possible and make only a brief distinction:

PURPOSES   Reasons why we are involved

GOALS   Broad general statements of what we are trying to accomplish

OBJECTIVES   Specific, measurable statements of what we want to accomplish by a given point in time.

In writing your objective you will follow these steps:

Translate your problem statement into an objective.

Check your objective to see if it is clear and complete.

Establish your criterion for success.

The definition of an objective is very similar to the definition of a problem. This should not be surprising, since the objective is basically to reduce or eliminate the problem.

An OBJECTIVE is...

1. A situation or condition
2. of people or the organization
3. that will exist in the future and
4. that is considered desirable
5. by the members of the organization.

There are several ways of distinguishing among types of objectives. Objectives may aim to solve a problem *external* to the organization, usually a problem of the community and/or target population, or they may aim to solve problems *internal* to the organization, such as employee training or motivation. Also, objectives may be directed to changing the skills, knowledge, or attitudes of *people*—for example, clients, customers, or staff—or they may aim at maintaining or changing a condition of the *community* or the *organization*. In our example, the personnel manager's objective will be to resolve a problem *internal* to the organization and to change a condition of the *organization*. Doing this may require changing the skills, knowledge, or attitudes of *people* in the organization.

STEP 2
A

Stating the problem as an objective

Your objective will include the same what, when, where, whom, and how much elements as the problem statement. However, there are these differences between the problem statement and the objective.

1. The problem states the situation in negative, undesirable terms, while the objective states a positive, desirable situation.

2. Since problems can rarely be completely eliminated, the size of the situation or condition is smaller in the statement of the objective. You will be limiting the objective to a realistic level that is still considered desirable by the people in your organization.

Here are two examples to illustrate the difference between problems and objectives.

The **problem** may be that 100 senior secretaries in the organization need to improve their shorthand skills. A realistic **objective** may be that 50 of them are able to increase their dictation speed from 80 words per minute to 100 words per minute with 90% accuracy in transcription. (This may be accomplished through more on-the-job practice, training, or other strategies.)

The **problem** may be that 200 students are experiencing personal or family crises. A realistic **objective** may be that 100 of them are able to resolve these crises. (This may occur as a result of program strategies such as counseling.)

STEP 2 A

Here are the problem statement and objective that the personnel manager has written.

SAMPLE PROBLEM

1. If something isn't done, six months from now

2. the city water department

3. will still not have a process for recruiting and promoting minorities and women

4. & 5. that has the support of all three employee unions, management, and six major community minority/women's advocate groups.

SAMPLE OBJECTIVE

1. As a result of this program, by July 1 of this year,

2. the city water department

3. will have a process for recruiting and promoting minorities and women

4. & 5. that has the support of at least two employee unions, management, and three major community minority/women's advocate groups.

Stating the problem as an objective

Now, write your problem statement from Step 1, and then translate it into your objective statement.

PROBLEM

OBJECTIVE

Is your objective really an objective?

Now you should check your objective and see if you can answer "yes" to the following questions. If so, you're ready to proceed. If not, you need to continue to refine your objective.

_____ 1. Is your objective stated as a declarative sentence?

_____ 2. Does your objective contain the what, when, where, whom, and how much elements from the problem statement?

_____ 3. Does your objective describe a future state, rather than an activity or process?

_____ 4. Have you limited the scope of your objective so that it is realistic?

Is your objective really an objective?

Here are some examples to illustrate the difference between objectives that fit our definition and those that don't.

DON'T SAY:

"The objective is *to provide* counseling services to 100 students."

INSTEAD, SAY:

"The objective is that 100 students will resolve a family or personal problem." (This may occur as the result of counseling or some other strategy.)

DON'T SAY:

"The objective is *to provide* training to 100 salespersons."

INSTEAD, SAY:

"The objective is that the salespersons in the department will increase their total sales by 10%." (This may occur as the result of training or some other strategy.)

STEP 2

C

Identifying criterion for success

This is the final check for your objective. You will be trying to answer the question: "How will I know when I have reached my objective?" If you can't identify your criterion for success, your objective probably isn't concrete enough. This is how the personnel manager did it.

A. SAMPLE PROBLEM

1. If something isn't done, six months from now

2. the city water department

3. will still not have a process for recruiting and promoting minorities and women

4. & 5. that has the support of all three employee unions, management, and six major community minority/women's advocate groups.

B. SAMPLE OBJECTIVE

1. As a result of this program, by July 1 of this year,

2. the city water department

3. will have a process for recruiting and promoting minorities and women

4. & 5. that has the support of at least two employee unions, management, and three major community minority/women's advocate groups.

C. SAMPLE CRITERION

The way I'll know I've met my objective is that the plan we send to the mayor by July 1 will be accompanied by a letter of endorsement from at least two employee unions, two major minority advocate groups, and one women's advocate group.

"If you don't know where you're going, how will you know when you've arrived?"

In the space below, write the evaluative criterion for the problem you defined in Step 1 of the planning process and the objective you developed earlier in Step 2. If you have trouble identifying your criterion for success, you need to go back to Step 1 and redefine your problem.

PROBLEM

OBJECTIVE

CRITERION

STEP 2
C

In this example, the personnel manager is working toward the objective of setting up a process for recruiting minorities and women that has the support of key groups inside and outside the department. However, if he had been writing the objective for the Affirmative Action Plan instead, it might have looked like this:

SAMPLE PLAN OBJECTIVE

1. A year from now

2. the water department

3. will have among its employees

4a. 30 percent women and 10 percent minorities,

4b. one-fifth of whom will be employed in the supervisory and technical levels of the organization,

5. and this will be accomplished with the support of employee unions.

If you are working with a plan objective, the steps in **Hip Pocket Guide** lay out most of the process you would use, for example, in writing a grant application for funding support or justifying a budget increase to your board of directors or your local government.

Identifying criterion for success

During the process of defining the problem and setting the objective, you probably noticed a significant change in the focus of the problem as perceived by the personnel manager. Had he seen his task as imposed from outside to accomplish some remote regulatory purpose and hadn't carefully thought through the problem definition, he might well have defined his problem like this:

SAMPLE PROBLEM

The department doesn't have an Affirmative Action Plan acceptable to the mayor.

SAMPLE OBJECTIVE

To write a new Affirmative Action Plan within six months.

SAMPLE CRITERION

I'll know I've been successful if the plan gets sent up to the mayor by the deadline.

If the personnel manager had taken this tack, the resulting strategy would probably have been quite different. Instead he has identified his own interests and the interests of the organization with those of the outside forces—the mayor, federal government regulations, minorities, and employee unions. In addition, he realizes that to implement the Affirmative Action Plan he must have the support of key groups from inside and outside the organization. As a result, the objective he has set is considerably more challenging and will involve skills in organizational change strategies. The personnel manager has been transformed from a bureaucrat doing just another paperwork task into a person attempting to make a significant change in the way his organization functions.

Before you begin Step 3, turn back to Parts A and B of the Epilogue (pp. 124–132) and review what you have learned about organizational change. Then read through Parts C and D of the Epilogue (pp. 133–143) so that you can begin thinking about how to get your plan accepted. You will go back to the Epilogue and work through Parts C and D more thoroughly after you have finished all six planning and evaluation steps.

CHOOSING AMONG ALTERNATE STRATEGIES

STEP 3

Now that you have defined your problem and set your objective, you can get to the business of figuring out how to solve the problem. Often at this stage, planners feel that they have done the hardest part (which is true) and that they can immediately start work on the solution (which isn't true). Three more planning processes are critical.

A List all the possible ways of reaching the objective.

B Analyze each alternative from several aspects to see how feasible it would be.

C Decide which alternative will be implemented.

In this step you will be listing and analyzing *strategies* or general approaches to reaching the objective. For a more formal definition—

A STRATEGY is...

1. A series or group of activities

2. that are carried out by members of the organization

3. to reach the desired objective.

How to get there...

This task may well be the most enjoyable part of planning. Now is the time to be creative, to cast reality to the winds—to forget that boards of directors, regulatory agencies, stubborn bosses, statutes, and traditions exist and to pretend that you have all the money and staff you need. We will at this stage list as many ideas as possible assuming that the more ideas we have, the better chance there will be of having a good one.

It's so easy, when faced with a problem, to jump immediately to some tried and true solution:

- Slow sales mean we need more advertising.

- Problem personnel need more supervision.

- Clients who don't fit agency policies get referred elsewhere.

- Students with problems get counseling.

The intent of this phase is to break away from all the standard solutions, to generate new ideas and new twists to old ideas. Remember the old maxim: "There is more than one way to skin a cat!"

The brainstorming process is one way to generate a lot of ideas in a hurry. In fifteen minutes a small group can often generate 50 to 100 ideas! Presented with an objective, the group thinks of as many strategies as possible for reaching the objective. There are three basic ground rules:

1. No criticism or evaluation of ideas is allowed. That only inhibits creativity.

2. Far out ideas are encouraged. They may trigger more practical ideas for someone else.

3. Don't hold back. Quantity is the main object. If you can't think of something, try a variation on someone else's idea.

This technique can be used with any group of people. One advantage of using "outsiders" to brainstorm strategies for reaching your objective is that it's always easier to solve someone else's problem. Outsiders will be less familiar with all the reasons why you can't do something.

STEP 3
A

Sample
List of Alternate Strategies

Once you have brainstormed a list of strategies, it may be possible to combine several of these ideas into one strategy; but for now we'll examine each of them as separate strategies.

SAMPLE OBJECTIVE

Process for recruiting and promoting minorities and women that has the support of employee unions and minority/women's advocate groups.

SAMPLE LIST OF ALTERNATE STRATEGIES

Copy Affirmative Action Plan (AAP) from other city departments or from other cities where it's been approved without conflict.

Write an AAP, and send to key groups for comment.

Committee of management and supervisory staff to write plan.

Committee of key employees and community advocates to write plan.

Ask community advocate groups to come up with a plan.

Attend union meetings, and ask for suggestions.

Ask union leaders for suggestions.

Ask a few employees who are my friends.

Ask for employee and advocate group suggestions first, then circulate plan for comment.

This page is for you to list as many possible alternate strategies as you can, from whatever source you like. You may want to use a brainstorming process with a group of people in your organization, or you may just want to ask people you see at a meeting if they have any ideas.

YOUR OBJECTIVE

LIST OF ALTERNATE STRATEGIES

STEP 3

B

Analyze each alternative from several aspects to see how feasible it would be.

How feasible are they?

Now that you have generated different strategies, here are three possible ways to analyze alternate strategies. At this point, you will look at each alternative from different perspectives. Think about how desirable each one may be without making a final decision about which one is best.

Most often, this part of planning is done intuitively. We reject certain strategies because we "know" they are too expensive or they "just won't work." The intent of these exercises is again to slow the process down, to allow a careful consideration of all the possibilities.

The three suggested techniques are:

1. A "force-field analysis" of forces in the environment which may help or hinder you in carrying out the strategy

2. A review of resources which would be needed for this strategy— which resources you have and which you can get

3. A check against a number of criteria you will use later in evaluating success.

To illustrate this process, the personnel manager will pick one of the strategies that resulted from his brainstorming process and analyze it using all three techniques. You will need to analyze several of your alternate strategies to see how they compare.

"...allow a careful consideration of all the possibilities."

1. Force-Field Analysis *

For the force-field analysis, imagine a straight, vertical line representing a tension between all the forces that would help you with this strategy (arrows pushing to the right) and all the forces that would get in your way (arrows pushing to the left).

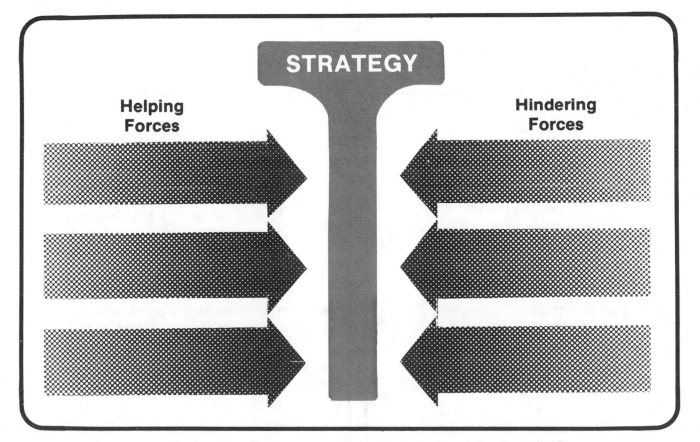

*Adapted from John E. Jones and J. William Pfeiffer (Eds.), *The 1973 Annual Handbook for Group Facilitators*. La Jolla, California: University Associates, 1973. Used with permission. It is based in part on materials developed by Warren Bennis and by Saul Eisen.

STEP 3
B

Sample
Force-Field Analysis

Here is how the personnel manager analyzed the helping and hindering forces for one strategy alternative:

SAMPLE OBJECTIVE

Process for recruiting and promoting minorities and women that has the support of employee unions and minority/women's advocate groups.

SAMPLE STRATEGY ALTERNATIVE

Form a task force representing key employees and advocate groups to develop an Affirmative Action Plan for the department.

HELPING FORCES

Interest in the problem has been recently expressed by advocate groups in the community.

One major employees' union has strong ties with outside unions that have a strong women's rights commitment.

Department director has expressed a willingness to try this approach.

There is a strong mandate from the mayor, the federal government, and others.

Public climate is currently favorable to equal opportunity as "the right thing to do."

HINDERING FORCES

We've never involved the community in solving internal problems.

Two of the unions have not been oriented to civil rights issues; one union has been strongly anti-civil rights.

Deputy director believes strongly in traditional hiring practices and strongly opposes quotas of any kind.

The employees will feel that something is being rammed down their throats.

There's a general public feeling that reverse discrimination isn't fair either; there's hostility to hiring and promoting people *because* they're minorities or women.

How feasible are they?

Force-Field Analysis

For practice, you can use the space below to do your own force-field analysis for one of the possible strategies you've thought of.

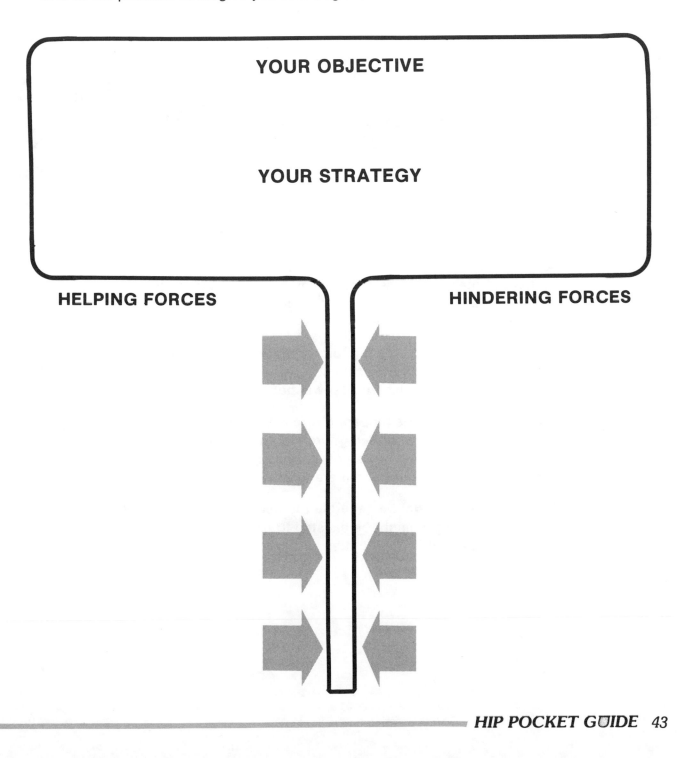

YOUR OBJECTIVE

YOUR STRATEGY

HELPING FORCES

HINDERING FORCES

STEP 3
B

Once these helping and hindering forces have been identified, you can ask a number of further questions. Careful work here will help you later when you plan the details of implementing your strategy in Step 4.

Sample
Analysis of Helping and Hindering Forces

1. **Do we have some influence over any of these forces? Which ones?**
   We have contacts with the outside union that has strong feminist ties. We may not be able to influence the strongly anti-civil rights union in our department.

2. **Can the effects of any helping forces be increased? How?**
   "Interest" expressed by advocate groups has been antagonistic; if we seek their cooperation, perhaps this interest will become more positive.

3. **Can the effects of some hindering forces be reduced?**
   The employees' feeling of being forced into something may be reduced if they can be represented in setting up the program and if it can be shown that "affirmative action" is in their interests too.

4. **What new forces might be generated to help carry out the strategy?**
   Community colleges might be enlisted to train future employees so we can have a pool of qualified minorities and women to recruit from.

How feasible are they?

Analysis of
Helping and Hindering Forces

On this page, you can consider these questions in relation to your own force-field analysis.

1. **Do we have some influence over any of these forces?**

2. **Can the effects of any helping forces be increased? How?**

3. **Can the effects of some hindering forces be reduced? How?**

4. **What new forces might be generated to help carry out the strategy?**

STEP 3
B

Now that you have examined all the forces acting for or against each strategy, you will have a better sense of the lay of the land and a good idea of which strategies are more or less feasible.

2. Review of Resources *

The second technique for considering the feasibility of each alternate strategy is to look at the resources that would be needed to carry out the strategy and think about which of these resources are *available* and which would need to be *acquired* in order to implement the strategy.

We usually think of resources as solid things, like money, people, buildings, equipment. There are many other less tangible resources, however, that can make or break a strategy. With all the money and staff in the world, a strategy won't work without the right combination of time, knowledge, skill, political influence, prestige, control over information, legitimacy, and sheer energy. All these "intangibles" should be considered resources too.

*The discussion and charts in this section are adapted from *Feasible Planning for Social Change* by Robert Morris and Robert H. Binstock, Columbia University Press, 1966. Used with permission.

How feasible are they?

Review of Resources

A formal definition is:

RESOURCES are...

1. Tangible things (like personnel, money, equipment, facilities)

2. and intangible things (like time, knowledge, skill, political influence, prestige, legitimacy, control over information, and energy)

3. used by an organization's personnel

4. to carry out a strategy or activity

5. that is designed to reach a desired objective.

The charts on the following pages provide a guide for considering what resources you will need to carry out each strategy. Following the sample chart, there is a blank for you to use in practice with one strategy.

STEP 3
B

Checklist for Consideration of Resource Needs

SAMPLE STRATEGY ALTERNATIVE

Form a task force representing key employees and advocate groups to develop an Affirmative Action Plan.

RESOURCE	Needed Resource Is this resource needed for this strategy? Yes/No	Resource Available Is it possible to divert resources to this strategy? Yes/No	Resource Not Available Is it possible to acquire this resource elsewhere? Yes/No
Personnel	Yes (administrative staff, task force representatives)	Yes	
Money	No		
Equipment	Yes (typewriter, xerox)		
Facilities	Yes (meeting room)	Yes	
Time	Yes (for research, meetings)	Yes	
Knowledge	Yes (Affirmative Action guidelines, personnel statistics)	Yes	
Skill	Yes (persuasion, leading meetings)	Yes	
Political Influence	Yes (getting key participants)		
Prestige (Reputation)	No		
Legitimacy	Yes (support of boss)	Yes	
Energy	Yes (to keep group at its task)	Yes	
Control over Information	Partial (department newsletter, memos to staff)	Yes	

How feasible are they?

Checklist for Consideration of Resource Needs

YOUR STRATEGY ALTERNATIVE

⬇ RESOURCE	Needed Resource Is this resource needed for this strategy? Yes/No	Resource Available Is it possible to divert resources to this strategy? Yes/No	Resource Not Available Is it possible to acquire this resource elsewhere? Yes/No
Personnel			
Money			
Equipment			
Facilities			
Time			
Knowledge			
Skill			
Political Influence			
Prestige (Reputation)			
Legitimacy			
Energy			
Control over Information			

STEP 3

B

3. Check Against Evaluative Criteria *

Now that you have considered each possible strategy in light of helping and hindering forces and the needed and available resources, there is a third technique for comparing alternate strategies: analyzing each alternative in terms of evaluative criteria that will be applied later to the plan itself. This means estimating how well you think each strategy would measure up according to these criteria:

1. **Appropriateness**—Is it "right" for you to use this kind of strategy? This question includes whether or not the strategy is appropriate to the organization's overall purpose and also whether the strategy is appropriate for anyone to use at all. An extreme example: most people would probably agree that mercy killing is not an appropriate strategy for eliminating the problem of potential dropouts and delinquents.

2. **Adequacy**—Given the size of the problem, will this strategy make enough of a difference to make it worth doing? For example, suppose there are 1,000 students with serious family and personal problems, and you have a strategy that will do a fantastic job of helping 10 of them. Is it worth doing?

How feasible are they?

Check Against Evaluative Criteria

3. **Effectiveness**—How successful will this strategy be in reaching the stated objective? For example, if the objective is that 100 students resolve a personal and family problem, would the strategy of counseling students really enable that many to resolve their problems? If the objective is that 100 secretaries will improve their shorthand skills, would the strategy of providing training in taking dictation and transcribing shorthand notes really enable them to do a better job? Might increased on-the-job practice of shorthand be just as effective or more effective?

4. **Efficiency**—How costly is the strategy compared to the benefits obtained? Are the benefits obtained worth the money and the other resources used? Do we get the most for our money? For example, if the costs of counseling are less than the costs resulting from future delinquency, then it is an "efficient" strategy. If the cost of training a sales force is more than the amount of projected future income from increased sales, then this is an "inefficient" strategy.

5. **Side effects**—What good and bad side effects might occur as a result of the strategy? For example, a bad side effect of counseling might be generating hostility in the parents toward the school, while a good side effect might be the students' improved performance in school. A bad side effect of implementing a new budgeting process might be an increase in staff reporting time, while a good side effect might be that more accurate or more detailed or more useful information is generated for use in upcoming budget requests.

*These evaluative criteria are adapted from a paper by Professor O. Lynn Deniston, "Evaluation of Disease Control Programs," Washington, D.C., U.S. Department of Health, Education and Welfare, Public Health Service, March, 1972.

STEP 3 B

The chart below provides a framework for considering these evaluative questions for each alternate strategy and for comparing strategies according to these evaluative criteria.

Sample
Review of
Evaluative Criteria

SAMPLE OBJECTIVE
Process for recruiting and promoting minorities and women that has the support of employee unions and minority/women's groups.

STRATEGY	Appropriate Yes/No/Maybe	Adequacy Hi/Med/Low	Effectiveness Hi/Med/Low	Efficiency Hi/Med/Low	Side Effects Good/Bad
ALTERNATIVE A: Develop task force of employees and advocates to write Affirmative Action Plan	Maybe	Hi	Hi	Med (probable benefits high, but so is cost)	**Good**—Precedent for better decision-making process. **Bad**—Precedent for too much citizen involvement; time-consuming.
ALTERNATIVE B: Ask for suggestions first, then circulate plan, ask for comments	Yes	Med	Med	Hi (probable benefits high, cost not so high)	**Good**—Precedent for more input in decision making. **Bad**—Hostility if we don't adopt their comments.
ALTERNATIVE C: Write plan, then circulate for comments	Yes	Low	Low	Med (probable benefits low, but so is cost)	**Good**—Avoid direct confrontation. **Bad**—Plan may not have real support.
ALTERNATIVE D: Copy plan from another city where it was implemented without conflict	Maybe	Low	Low	Low (low cost, but low benefit too)	**Good**—Maybe no one would know we'd done a plan! **Bad**—Plan might never be used by department.

How feasible are they?

Review of Evaluative Criteria

In the space below, rate each of your possible strategies according to these evaluative criteria. At this point, all you will need is a "guesstimate" of how well the strategy measures up.

YOUR OBJECTIVE

⬇ STRATEGY	Appropriate Yes/No/Maybe	Adequacy Hi/Med/Low	Effectiveness Hi/Med/Low	Efficiency Hi/Med/Low	Side Effects Good/Bad
ALTERNATIVE A:					
ALTERNATIVE B:					
ALTERNATIVE C:					
ALTERNATIVE D:					

STEP 3
C

Decide which alternative will be implemented.

Decision-making Concerns

You have now painstakingly listed all the possible alternate ways to meet your objective. You have analyzed each alternative and made comparisons based on helping or hindering forces, resources needed, and evaluative criteria.

With all this information available, you should now be able to come to some reasonable decision. But **who** will make the decision? **How** will the decision be made? The answers depend on the decision-making structure of the organization and the type of decision to be made.

Who makes the decision?

In some organizations and in some situations, the decision will be made uni-laterally by the supervisor, manager, or president.

> The manager may decide without staff input, without explaining the problem or asking for opinions about how to solve it: "Here's what I want you to do."

> Or, the manager may make the decision after asking for others' opinions: "I'm thinking about doing it this way. What's your reaction?" The manager may or may not consider these opinions in making the decision.

In other organizations or other situations, the decision will be made by a group.

> The manager may present a problem to a group and ask them to decide how to solve it: "I'll abide by whatever you decide to do."

> Or, the group may both define the problem and decide what to do about it. A staff member says: "I think we have a problem here. What do you think? What shall we do about it?"

Each of these decision-making styles is appropriate at various times and for various kinds of decisions. Probably the best time to use group decision making is when a high level of involvement and commitment by group members will be needed to implement the decision being made.

When using a group to make a decision, here are some basic guidelines to follow:

1. Use a group when the acceptance of the solution by the group is at least as important as the quality of the decision to be made. For example: a new approach to handling community relations or a new method of budgeting.

2. Set clear limits on the boundaries of the decision you want the group to consider. For example: *within a budget of $2,000,* what is the best way to solve this problem?

3. Make it clear whether you are *asking the group for suggestions* on how to solve the problem or whether you are *delegating the decision* itself to the group.

How is the decision to be made?

Within a group setting, there are many ways to reach a decision—some more common than others.*

1. *"Plop" decision*—Various suggestions are bypassed without response. One proposal is finally agreed upon, but most members feel their ideas have "plopped."

2. *Decision by authority rule*—The group discusses an issue, but the group leader or someone else in authority makes the decision.

3. *Decision by minority*—One or several people railroad a proposal through without giving opponents an opportunity to be heard.

4. *Decision by majority rule*—A poll or vote is taken. The majority go away satisfied, but some are unsatisfied and may not cooperate in implementing the proposal.

5. *Consensus decision*—Discussion continues until a decision is reached that everyone can accept and support.

6. *Unanimous decision*—Everyone really agrees on the action to be taken.

Again, each of these techniques may be appropriate for some situations. Some are more efficient and less time-consuming. Others take more time, but when high commitment and involvement are needed, the extra time may be well spent.

Most people have a lot of experience with group decision by "plop," authority, and minority and majority rule. That is why you should practice using the consensus approach in your organization when you work through the process of listing alternate strategies, analyzing them, and choosing the one to be used.

The excerpt on the following page is a good description of decisions by consensus. It includes some guidelines for group use.

*The six types of group decision making summarized here are adapted, by permission, from *Process Consultation: Its Role in Organization Development,* by Edgar H. Schein. Copyright 1969 by Addison-Wesley Publishing Co., Inc., Reading, Mass. The classification is patterned after a formulation first proposed by Robert Blake.

STEP 3

C

What is decision by consensus? *

Consensus is a decision process for making full use of available resources and for resolving conflicts creatively. Consensus is difficult to reach, so not every ranking will meet with everyone's *complete* approval. Complete unanimity is not the goal—it is rarely achieved. But each individual should be able to accept the group rankings on the basis of logic and feasibility. When all group members feel this way, you have reached consensus as defined here, and the judgment may be entered as a group decision. This means, in effect, that you can block the group if you think it's necessary; at the same time, you should use this option in the best sense of reciprocity. Here are some guidelines to use in achieving consensus:

1. Avoid arguing for your own rankings. Present your position as lucidly and logically as possible, but listen to the other members' reactions and consider them carefully before you press your point.

2. Do not assume that someone must win and someone must lose when discussion reaches a stalemate. Instead, look for the next-most-acceptable alternative for all parties.

3. Do not change your mind simply to avoid conflict and to reach agreement and harmony. When agreement seems to come too quickly and easily, be suspicious. Explore the reasons and be sure everyone accepts the solution for basically similar or complementary reasons. Yield only to positions that have objective and logically sound foundations.

4. Avoid conflict-reducing techniques such as majority vote, averages, coin-flips, and bargaining. When dissenting members finally agree, don't feel that they must be rewarded by having their own way on some later point.

5. Differences of opinion are natural and expected. Seek them out and try to involve everyone in the decision process. Disagreements can help the group's decision because with a wide range of information and opinions, there is a greater chance that the group will hit upon more adequate solutions.

*From "Decisions, Decisions, Decisions," by Jay Hall. REPRINTED BY PERMISSION OF PSYCHOLOGY TODAY MAGAZINE. Copyright © 1971, Ziff-Davis Publishing Company.

Why is this the best decision?

No matter who makes the decision or how it is made, it is important to be explicit about the reasons for making that choice, just as it is important to be clear about what the problem and objective are. The analysis of helping and hindering forces, resources needed, and check against evaluative criteria have provided you with many reasons for making a decision among the alternatives. Often the reasons for a decision are "gut reactions," which may or may not coincide with a more carefully thought out rationale. For example:

1. **Organization constraints**—"We don't have enough money or staff time to do anything else."

2. **People required for implementation**—"We could never get the people in the other section to cooperate on this."

3. **Location of resistance**—"I'll buck my staff but not my boss."

4. **Visibility**—"I know we wouldn't serve a lot of people doing this, but we'd get great press coverage."

5. **Possibility of success**—"This option isn't the most effective, but I know we can do it."

—Or simply

6. **Personal choice**—"I would rather do this."

"Best" strategies for any organization change from time to time and from issue to issue, but it is important at any time to have a method for weighing the alternatives and to be able to state the *rationale* for the final choice.

On the following page is the sample rationale for selecting one of the alternate strategies for developing an Affirmative Action Plan.

Sample
Rationale for Selection
of Alternate Strategy

MEMO

TO: Department Director
FROM: Personnel Manager
RE: Recommended Strategy for Developing Affirmative Action Plan

As you suggested, I have analyzed several possible strategies for developing an Affirmative Action Plan within the next six months that has the support of employee and community advocate groups. Based on my analysis and conversations with other key people in the department, I would recommend Alternative A—forming a task force representing employee unions and minority and women's advocate groups to develop the plan.

Briefly, my reasons for recommending this course are as follows:

1. Based on the evaluative criteria, I eliminated Alternatives C and D on the grounds of low effectiveness and adequacy. (However, time constraints, lack of energy, or unwillingness to risk failure might make one of these more feasible.)

2. If it worked, Alternative A would be more effective than B, but the analysis of helping and hindering forces makes it clear that this alternative would be very difficult to pull of successfully. However, if it *were* successful, there would be two potentially good side effects: assurance of support from the employees within the department and a better decision-making process for the department. This should outweigh the bad side effect of more time spent in making decisions.

3. Looking at resources required, I find that the necessary resources *are* available to do Alternative A. In terms of efficiency there would be a high cost in time, but this could be justified if the strategy worked and the potentially high benefits were achieved.

4. The appropriateness of Alternative A is questionable; some will object to involving outside citizen advocates in the department's decision making.

With these factors understood, I suggest we go ahead with Alternative A. I know it will be controversial, but I've had indications of support from a few key people. Therefore, I feel we'd be justified in committing the necessary time and energy resources because the potential benefits are well worth the risk involved. If you agree, I'll begin immediately to work out a detailed schedule for implementing the strategy.

Decision-making Concerns

Rationale for Selection of Alternate Strategy

Write a memo to your supervisor using the space below to recommend how to implement your plan and to discuss your rationale for this choice.

MEMO

TO:

FROM:

RE:

STEP 4

The motto of the first two steps in planning was: "If you don't know where you want to go, you'll never know when you arrive." In Steps 3 and 4 the motto is: "The more you know about where you're going, the closer you are to being there." In Step 3 you decided on one or more general strategies that you thought would be the "best" way of arriving at your objective. In Step 4, you'll move farther away from abstractions and get down to the real "nitty-gritty" of who is actually going to do what, on what days, with whom, and with what resources. If this dose of reality tells you that you have stated the problem inaccurately or that your beautifully analyzed strategy just won't work, you may have to go back and rethink Steps 1 through 3.

At the end of Step 4, you will know what major events will take place over a certain period of time, who will have major responsibility, and what specific resources will be needed. For some of the initial activities, you will have defined even more specifically what tasks have to be done, by whom, and on what day of the week.

Before getting down to reality, let's recap where you have been so far: defined the problem, stated the objective, and decided among alternate strategies. The following sample reviews these steps and looks ahead to Step 4.

STEP 1   **Sample Problem:** If nothing is done, the department will not have a process for recruiting and promoting minorities and women that has the support of employee and advocate groups.

STEP 2   **Sample Objective:** By July 1, the department will have a process for recruiting and promoting minorities and women that has the support of employee and advocate groups.

STEP 3   **Sample Strategy:** Form a task force representing employee and advocate groups to develop the Affirmative Action Plan.

STEP 4   **Sample Activity:** Get representatives of key groups to agree to serve on a task force.

Sample Task: Make a list of potential task force members. Schedule appointments with each.

As usual, the process of preparing to implement activities can be divided into a number of handy steps.

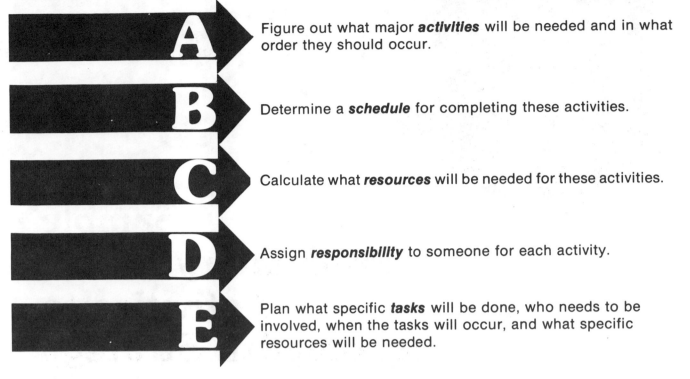

A Figure out what major *activities* will be needed and in what order they should occur.

B Determine a *schedule* for completing these activities.

C Calculate what *resources* will be needed for these activities.

D Assign *responsibility* to someone for each activity.

E Plan what specific *tasks* will be done, who needs to be involved, when the tasks will occur, and what specific resources will be needed.

Before you start, here are some more definitions to help clarify what we are talking about.

An ACTIVITY is...

1. A specific procedure or process
2. completed at a certain point in time
3. that is carried out by organization personnel
4. as part of a strategy
5. for reaching the desired objective.

A task is mostly just a "little activity," but here is a more formal definition:

A TASK is...

1. A specific procedure or process,
2. including what will be done, when, and by whom,
3. that is part of a larger "activity."

Now you can begin identifying what needs to be done to implement your plan.

STEP 4
A

Figure out what major *activities* will be needed and in what order they should occur.

Sample
Preliminary List of Activities to Accomplish Strategy

At this point, you are starting with a strategy—a certain way of approaching the problem. But what **activities** need to be done to carry out the strategy? Start by making a rough list of possible activities. Look back at your force-field analysis of helping and hindering forces in Step 3 for ideas.

Below is the personnel manager's preliminary list of activities. There is space on the opposite page for you to list your own activities.

SAMPLE STRATEGY

Form task force to develop Affirmative Action Plan.

SAMPLE LIST OF ACTIVITIES

- Get members to serve on task force.
- Arrange task force meeting.
- Get task force agreement on general content plan.
- Task force members get input from groups that they represent.
- Get letters of support from employee and advocate groups.
- Type rough draft of plan.

Preliminary List of Activities
to Accomplish Strategy

YOUR STRATEGY

LIST OF ACTIVITIES

STEP 4

A

Planning Activities

Next you need to order these activities in a sequence. One way to do this—and at the same time to check to be sure that you've thought of everything—is to start at the end and think backward, asking a series of questions: "If this is where I want to be, what do I have to do *just before* I get to this point?" "All right, then, what do I have to do just before I get to that point?"

To illustrate, take the way the personnel manager thought backward in our sample problem.

a. We've defined our objective as an Affirmative Action Plan having the support of both employee and advocate groups, and we've said this will be done in six months (by July 1).

   We've decided our strategy for reaching this objective is to develop the plan through a representative task force.

b. Now, if we want the plan completed by July 1, using this strategy, what has to happen *just before* that?
   Answer: The final plan has to be typed and duplicated and letters of support obtained from employee and advocate groups.

c. What has to happen *just before* that?
   Answer: The task force has to agree on the final draft, after feedback is received from the groups represented.

d. And *before that,* someone has to draft a plan for review by task force members and their groups.

e. And *before that,* the task force has to agree on the general content.

f. And *before that,* the employee and advocate groups and management must identify their interests and concerns and convey them to the task force members.

And so on, back to the point where you currently are in planning. We've assumed here that the department director has made the decision to follow this strategy and given the personnel manager the go-ahead.

The chart on the next page illustrates the major activities that have been identified for the sample plan. Notice that two further refinements have been made on the chart.

1. At point (b), two activities that will occur simultaneously are shown in two boxes lined up vertically.

2. There are three horizontal rows of boxes— the top is used for STAFF activities, such as writing and typing the draft report; the middle, for activities of the TASK FORCE; and the botton, for activities involving the GROUPS represented on the task force.

Try to think of these activities as building blocks hooked together in such a way (with arrows on the sample chart) that they lead to the desired outcome.

Following the sample chart is a blank page for you to use to identify the major activities in your strategy by thinking backward from the objective you have defined. If you are involving different work groups in your strategy, indicate which activities will be performed by what groups as in the sample.

STEP 4

A

66

Sample

Major Activities Planned to Carry Out Selected Strategy

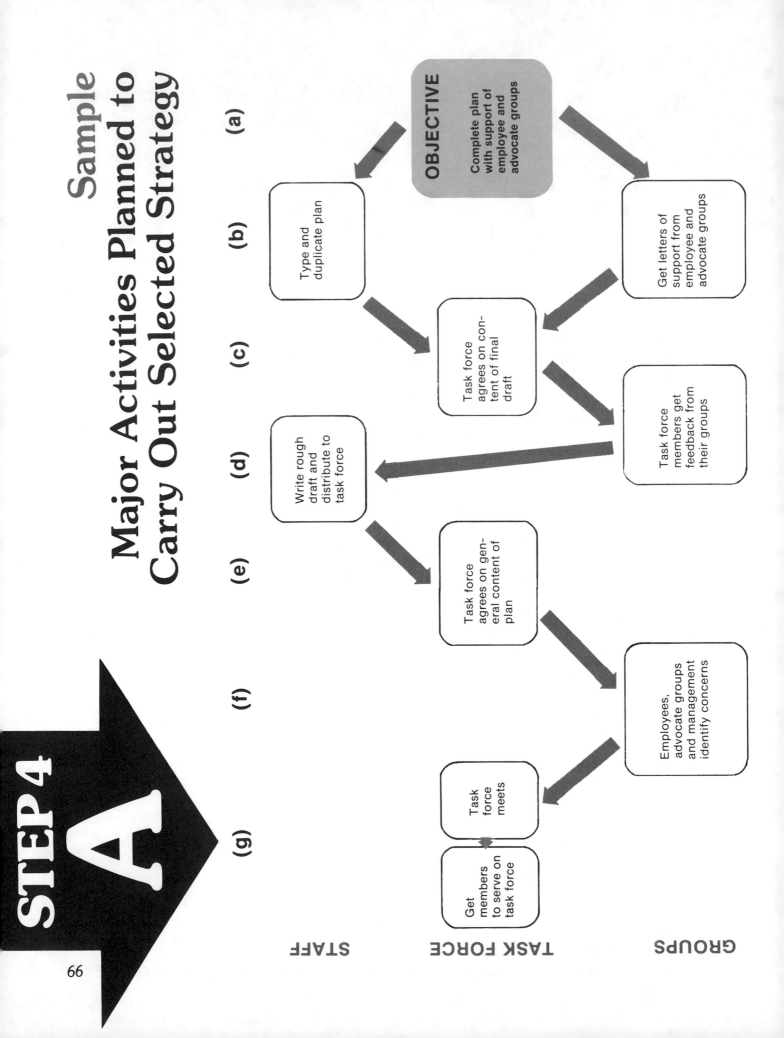

(a)   (b)   (c)   (d)   (e)   (f)   (g)

STAFF

TASK FORCE

GROUPS

OBJECTIVE

Complete plan with support of employee and advocate groups

Type and duplicate plan

Get letters of support from employee and advocate groups

Task force agrees on content of final draft

Task force members get feedback from their groups

Write rough draft and distribute to task force

Task force agrees on general content of plan

Employees, advocate groups and management identify concerns

Task force meets

Get members to serve on task force

Major Activities Planned to Carry Out Selected Strategies

OBJECTIVE

(a)

(b)

(c)

(d)

(e)

(f)

(g)

STEP 4

B

Deadlines & Schedules

Once these activities have been identified, the next step is to set some general deadlines for completing each activity. At this step, you are beginning to assess how much time each stage will take in order to complete the entire process in the desired time. This means two things:

1. Stating the activity in the form of the process *to be completed* by a certain point. For example, the personnel manager will write on his schedule, "Final draft typed and duplicated," rather than "Type and duplicate final draft." By stating the task in this form it is easier to answer the test question, "How will I know when I've completed this activity?"

   (If this sounds familiar, it's because you did the same thing in defining the objective as a future state, rather than as a verb. Now, at the activity stage, you're really setting "mini-objectives" for the completion of each activity.)

2. Placing the activities into a calendar form as illustrated on page 72. This process will show you clearly where one or more activities have to be completed before the next activity can begin.

After completing this process of identifying activities and setting deadlines, it's often a good idea to make the whole process public. One way to do this is by posting it on a large chart on the office wall. There are several reasons for doing this:

1. It allows everyone to have a common understanding of what the major stages are and and what is to be completed by a certain time.

2. It provides a constant reminder of how much has already been accomplished (a little "pat on the back" for the group) and how much is left to do.

3. It helps people focus energies on the priority activities that have been identified, instead of getting lost in the details.

4. It increases the chances that people will re-evaluate where they are in the process as time goes on and make revisions if things don't work out as planned. (They often don't!)

68

There are many techniques for scheduling activities. Three of the more common ones are shown before you get to the technique modified for **Hip Pocket Guide.**

1. SCHED-U-GRAPH® Technique

This is a simple tool for scheduling activities and projects, developed by the Sperry Rand Corporation. The instrument is a chart (24" x 42") containing pockets for 3" x 5" cards. The horizontal portion of the chart is labeled by month and the specific activities or tasks are typed on 3" x 5" cards and inserted in the appropriate slots.

For example, if you were preparing a budget for presentation to the Board of Directors in November, you would identify the various activities or duties involved and the approximate time to begin and complete them.

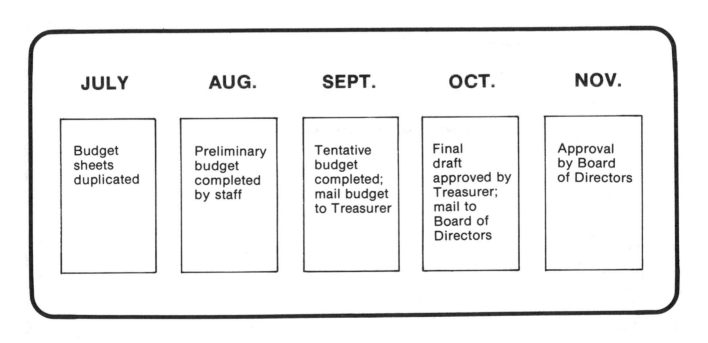

JULY	AUG.	SEPT.	OCT.	NOV.
Budget sheets duplicated	Preliminary budget completed by staff	Tentative budget completed; mail budget to Treasurer	Final draft approved by Treasurer; mail to Board of Directors	Approval by Board of Directors

This technique helps you see what needs to be done in a general time frame, but it has some weaknesses. It is difficult to determine the time needed to complete the tasks, and you may schedule more tasks than can be accomplished during any one particular month. Furthermore, it is impossible to show any relationship among the various activities and tasks.

SCHED-U-GRAPH is a registered trademark of the Sperry Rand Corporation.

Gantt Scheduling

In this method, a bar chart is used to reflect completion dates and activities. Horizontal dotted lines are drawn so their lengths are proportional to the planned duration of each activity. Progress on each activity is monitored by drawing solid lines parallel to and below the dotted lines to show actual duration for completed activities.

Activity	July 6 13 20 27	August 3 10 17 24 31	September 7 14 21 28	October 5 12 19 26	November 3 10 17
Budget sheets duplicated	– – – – –				
Staff briefed	– – – – – –				
Preliminary budget completed by staff		– – – – – – – – –			
Tentative budget completed					
Budget mailed to Treasurer		– – – – – – – –			
Final draft approved by Treasurer				· – – – – –	
Mailed to Board of Directors					– – – –
Approved by Board of Directors					– – – – –

Activities are listed in the first column on the left. To use the Gantt technique in the "forward direction" you work from left to right, plotting activities as they must occur over time in relation to other activities and establishing a completion date for the job. Still, the relationships between the various activities are not completely clear.

3. PERT Chart*

PERT-charting is a more sophisticated technique, developed by the U.S. government for keeping track of such intricate processes as building submarines. This technique is used when it is necessary for many tasks to be accomplished in sequence and in the shortest possible time. It is a technique well-suited to group planning, where cooperation is essential to get many tasks done by a given deadline.

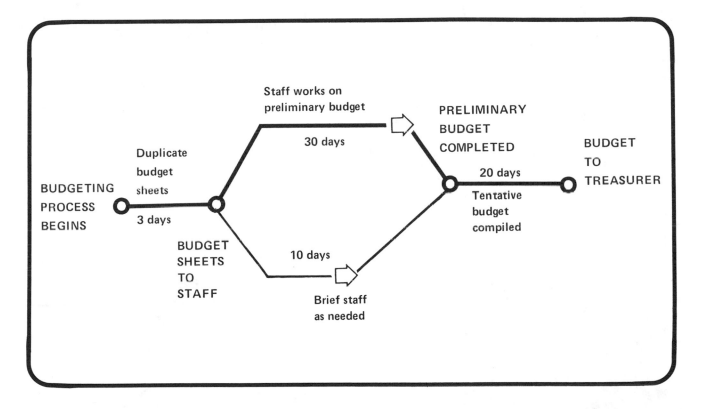

The PERT chart identifies *activities,* which culminate in *events.* Working backward from the final deadline, the time needed for each activity is calculated, and deadlines are scheduled for each event. By showing activities that can occur simultaneously and those that must occur in sequence, the chart reveals a *critical path,* which is the overall time needed to complete the project. An advantage of PERT is that it helps the group members focus their energies on critical tasks and continually re-evaluate the process to see if they are on schedule.

A simple PERT chart is illustrated above, with the critical path shown as a heavy line.

*PERT stands for Program Evaluation and Review Technique.

STEP 4

B

Sample

Schedule for Completing Major Activities

The personnel manager has used a modified PERT technique. He's already identified his key activities and ordered them in sequence by thinking backward from the objective (pp. 64–66). Now he needs to figure out how much time each activity will take and establish deadlines for the completion of each activity. In this illustration the boxes represent *events* or completed activities, and the arrows represent *activities* in process over the indicated time period. The blank is for you to use in arranging your major activities into a calendar format.

INTERMEDIATE DATES

							TARGET DATE
Feb. 1	Feb. 15	(10 weeks*) ⇨ May 1	May 15	June 1	June 15	June 30	July 1

STAFF

- Members have agreed to serve on task force
- Rough draft typed and distributed to task force
- Plan typed and duplicated

TASK FORCE

- Task force has met
- Task force has agreed on general content of plan
- Task force has agreed on content of final draft
- Task force members have received feedback from groups

OBJECTIVE

Plan completed with support of employee and advocate groups

GROUPS

- Employee and advocate groups and management identify concerns*
- Letters of support received from employee and advocate groups

*Ideally, task force members would plan a detailed strategy for obtaining

Schedule for Completing Major Activities

TARGET DATE

INTERMEDIATE DATES

Indicate dates

OBJECTIVE

STEP 4
C

Sample Resources Needed (or Budget)

Now that the major activities have been laid out in calendar form, it is possible to determine what resources will be needed to carry out the strategy. The primary things to consider at this point are: how much staff time will be needed, and what other costs are involved? A general or detailed budget may be drawn up at this point too.

For the sample strategy, here are the estimated resources needed:

SAMPLE STRATEGY

Form a task force representing employee and advocate groups to develop an Affirmative Action Plan.

Sample Resources	Six-Month Budget January–June
Personnel manager @ $20,000/yr. plus 20% fringes, ¼ time for 6 months	$ 3,000
Shift personnel manager's routine tasks to administrative assistant @ $18,000/yr. plus 20% fringes, ¼ time for 6 months	2,700
Clerical time @ $4.50/hour average 10 hrs./week for 6 months	1,170
Miscellaneous (supplies, printing, telephone, travel)	200
Conference room 4 hrs./week for 6 months	–0–
TOTAL COST	$ 7,070

Resources Needed
(or Budget)

After identifying what you'll need in actual dollars and cents, you may want to look at the strategy again and check to be sure it's really worth it. Here's some space for you to list the resources needed for your strategy

STRATEGY

Resources   **Budget**

STEP 4
D

Assign *responsibility* to someone for each activity.

Sample
Assignment
of Responsibility

After figuring out the costs involved and deciding to go ahead with the strategy, the next step is to assign responsibility for each of the major activities. The person who's responsible will then proceed with even more detailed planning of how to do that activity.

In the sample strategy, responsibility might be divided as follows:

Activity	Who's Responsible	Completion Date
1. Contacting potential task force representatives and getting their commitment to serve	Department director, assisted by personnel manager	February 1
2. Arranging meetings of task force	Personnel manager, assisted by clerical staff	February 15
3. Identifying interests and concerns of employees, management, and advocate groups	Task force members; personnel manager responsible for management interests and concerns	May 1
4. Writing and distributing rough draft	Personnel manager, assisted by clerical staff	May 15
5. Getting feedback from groups represented on task force	Task force members; personnel manager responsible for management feedback	June 1
6. Typing and duplicating final draft	Clerical staff, supervised by personnel manager	June 30
7. Getting letters of support from employee and advocate groups	Task force members	June 30

Note that this exercise will pay off later when the potential task force members are contacted. The department director will be able to tell them exactly what will be expected of them if they agree to serve on the task force.

Assignment of Responsibility

This space is for you to use in assigning responsibility for each major activity.

Activity	Who's Responsible	Completion Date

Plan what specific *tasks* will be done, who needs to be involved, when the tasks will occur, and what specific resources will be needed.

STEP 4

E

Task Planning

Once major activities have been assigned, the responsible staff member proceeds to detail precisely what has to be done, by whom, how, and when. One way to do this is, again, to work backward from the desired end point. Along the way, you may find that you have thought of other major activities that should be part of this strategy or that are part of another strategy for meeting this objective.

Returning to the example, you've seen that the personnel manager has been assigned responsibility for most of the main activities. At this point, he is ready to plan in detail the tasks for completing the first major activity—getting commitment of key representatives to serve on the task force.

The worksheet on the following page shows his detailed plan. After that, there is a blank page that you can use to practice doing detailed planning for one of your major activities.

STEP 4 E

Task Planning Sheet

Sample

RESPONSIBLE STAFF MEMBER: Personnel Manager

Strategy: Form task force to develop Affirmative Action Plan.
Activity: Get agreement of members to serve on task force.

TASKS	Why?	When?	Who?	Resources
1. List key groups and potential task force members.	Make sure all possibilities are considered.	Jan. 3	Self	3 hrs.
2. Go over list with department director and agree on whom to approach	Get director's perspective and approval.	Jan. 4	Self, Department director	2 hrs.
3. Review overall strategy with department director.	Make sure we're on the same wavelength, confirm commitment to strategy.	Jan. 4	Self, Department director, Clerical	(same as # 2)
4. Arrange lunch meetings with some potential members for preliminary discussion; department director will contact others directly.	Person-to-person, informal approach most likely to succeed.	Jan. 5 – Jan. 12	Self, Department director	6 hrs.
5. Attend these preliminary meetings with each potential member and department director.	Get their commitment to serve on task force.	Jan. 15 – 22	Self, Department director	12 hrs.
6. Possibly arrange to meet with some employee and/or advocate groups to explain reasons for task force.	Deal with possible problems early in the game.	Jan. 22 – 29	Self	15 hrs.
7. Follow up contacts with those who weren't sure or get alternates if they said no.	Make sure key groups are represented by someone.	Jan. 22 – 29	Self	6–8 hrs.
8. Send letters inviting them to be on task force and notifying them of first meeting in two weeks.	Official recognition; time to get meeting on their calendar.	Feb. 1	Self, Clerical	4 hrs.

Task Planning Sheet

RESPONSIBLE STAFF MEMBER: _____

Your Strategy:

Your Activity:

TASKS	Why?	When?	Who?	Resources?

DESIGNING THE EVALUATION

STEP 5

You started this whole process of planning because you had "evaluated" a situation in the community or in the organization and had identified a problem that needed to be solved. You decided that your objective would be to reduce this problem by a certain amount. Then, you defined a strategy and a number of activities through which you would reach the objective. Finally, you determined what resources would be needed to carry out the strategy and activities.

Now you need a step that will tell you, on an ongoing basis, how well you are doing at solving the problem that you started with. Also, you'll want to be able to make decisions about the plan as you go along, and you'll want to provide feedback to those who are implementing the plan. These are the three basic reasons for doing evaluation.

1. Evaluation to Monitor Performance

This is one important reason for doing evaluation. You want to know whether your program (defined as resources, activities, and strategies) is making an impact in reducing the problem as you had planned. As you implement the plan, you will learn more about the problem and may have to rethink your objective. Assuming the objective continues to be realistic and appropriate, you will want to check out each aspect of the plan periodically to see whether any adjustments need to be made to keep the plan "on course" in reaching the objective.

If everything is going smoothly, *resources* are combined with *activities*, which add up to a *strategy* (or strategies), which results in the *objective* being met:

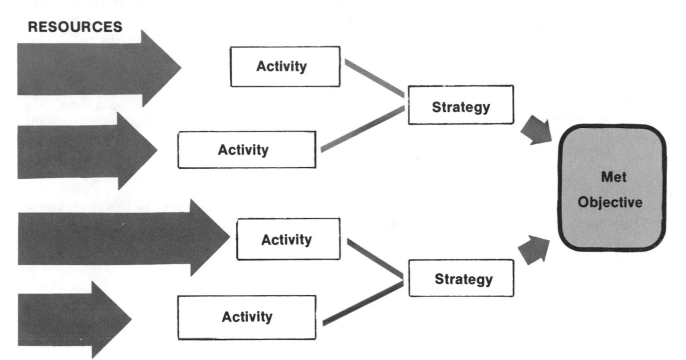

RESOURCES

So you can see that planning and evaluation are closely woven together. Planning is incomplete unless you have some way of knowing whether or not the plan is working, and evaluation is pointless unless there is some standard by which to determine what is "success" or "failure," "good" or "bad" performance.

2. Evaluation to Make Decisions

Another reason for doing evaluation is to provide a source of information that can be used to make decisions about the program. Keeping the problem and objective always in mind, you will continually be making decisions that should keep you on target: Do you need to adjust the "mix" of resources you are using? Will it take more resources to do this effectively at all? Should you try another strategy or modify this one? Finally, should you drop this plan altogether?

3. Evaluation to Give Feedback to Staff

Still another purpose of evaluation, which is too often overlooked, is to provide feedback to those who are implementing the plan. Information about how well we are doing is an important source of motivation, satisfaction, and personal growth for all of us. A good evaluation process should provide this information.

In Step 5 you will design an evaluation system that will provide information for comparing actual performance with planned performance and for making decisions about the plan. In Step 6, you will consider further the use of evaluative information in decision making. You will also consider evaluation as feedback to those involved in implementing the plan.

Before you look at some ways to think about and design an evaluation process, note that it is not suggested that you *start* doing evaluation. Everyone evaluates all the time. Everyone continually makes decisions—consciously or unconsciously—based on the key evaluation questions: "How well am I doing?" or "How well is this working?" However, better information may lead to better decisions. This step includes some ways of turning intuitive feelings into something that can be measured and making evaluation more explicit and systematic and thereby more available to all who are working on the project.

This step is *not* about evaluation as filling out forms for their own sake or to satisfy some outside funding or regulatory organization whose objectives we either don't know or don't accept. Rather, evaluation is feedback to people who are implementing strategies to meet objectives they have set for themselves or to meet someone else's objectives that they have agreed to accept.

Here are the five basic steps in preparing an evaluation design.

A Anticipate what **decisions** might have to be made about the plan along the way.

B Look at each part of the plan and anticipate where a **comparison** of actual performance and planned performance might yield information that will help make key decisions.

C Design **measures** of appropriateness, adequacy, effectiveness, efficiency, and side effects in order to compare actual and planned performance.

D Figure out how to obtain the **data** for these measurements.

E Determine who will **analyze** the data, how, and when.

Through the planning process (Steps 1 through 4), you have identified a problem, set an objective, and planned strategies, activities, and resources. Here is a preview of what the completed evaluation design (Steps 5 and 6) will include:

1. Review of decisions that might need to be made

2. Description of possible breakdowns between actual and planned performance

3. Set of measures to be used in comparing actual and planned performance

4. List of sources from which data will be gathered

5. Plan for how the data will be analyzed and who will do it

6. Plan for how evaluative information will be used in the organization (Step 6)

STEP 5

A

Anticipate what *decisions* might have to be made about the plan along the way.*

Decision Points!

As you move through the process of implementing your plan, you will continually be making decisions about it. These decisions fall into four basic categories:

1. Do we need to adjust the "mix" of resources?

2. Will it take more resources to do this at all?

3. Should we try another strategy or modify this one?

4. Finally, the ultimate go/no-go decision, should we drop this plan altogether?

To see how these decisions might need to be made at any point as the plan is implemented, look at the flow chart on the opposite page. You'll recognize that this chart is from Step 4. Two key decision points highlighted on the chart will be analyzed by the personnel manager.

*These decision points were identified for the author by Professor George E. Johnson at the Institute for Public Policy Studies, University of Michigan.

Decision Points!

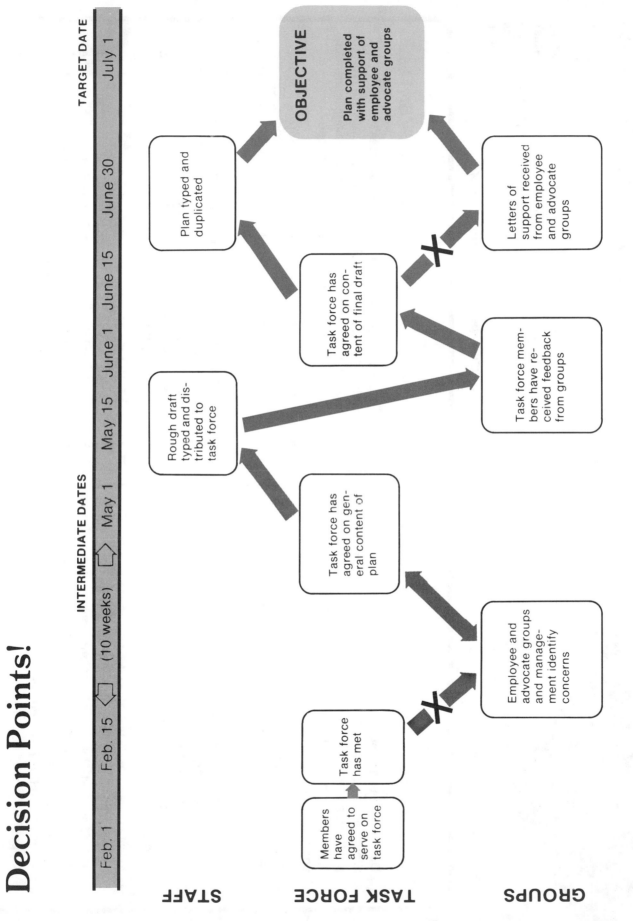

STEP 5

Sample
Decision Points!

Now, let's assume that the plan has been implemented successfully up until June. The key groups have all been represented on the task force, and it's been meeting frequently. Now in mid-June, the personnel manager finds that only one of the smaller employee groups is willing to endorse the plan worked out by the task force. What decisions might need to be made at this point?

SAMPLE LATER DECISION POINTS

1. **Do we need to adjust the mix of resources?**
   Maybe the department director needs to take a more active leadership role at this point, rather than leaving implementation entirely up to the personnel manager.

2. **Will it take more resources to do this at all?**
   Maybe it's just not realistic to think the process can be completed in six months. Maybe we would try to get a three-month extension.

3. **Should we try another strategy or modify this one?**
   The task force has worked well up to a point, but maybe another strategy for obtaining widespread employee and advocate support must be tried now. (Back to the brainstorming stage!)

4. **Should we drop the plan altogether?**
   Again, maybe it's just impossible to get broad support for an Affirmative Action Plan. Maybe it will just have to be imposed upon the organization by management with the hope that attitudes will change later.

By the end of February, the personnel manager finds that a key employee group has not agreed to support the strategy. What decisions need to be made?

SAMPLE DECISION POINTS

1. **Do we need to adjust the "mix" of resources?**
   Would some political influence help? Maybe someone from another employee group that is supportive can talk to the resisting ones. (Refer back to the analysis of helping and hindering forces.)

2. **Will it take more resources to do this at all?**
   Maybe it's just a matter of more time and more meetings with the resisting group. Can we afford to take more time?

3. **Should we try another strategy or modify this one?**
   Maybe the employee group is resisting because it doesn't want outside advocates on the task force. Maybe the task force could just be made up of employee and management representatives.

4. **Should we drop the plan altogether?**
   Our objective was to write an Affirmative Action Plan that has the support of key employee and community groups. Without the backing of this one group, maybe that objective just can't be reached now. Maybe we'll have to do an Affirmative Action Plan administratively and hope the support will come later.

Decision Points!

With these examples as guides, use this page to jot down the kind of decisions you might be making about your plan somewhere along the line. Also, you might want to anticipate at what point during implementation you would want to make these decisions. Look back at your activity flow chart from Step 4 on page 73. This will help you locate potential decision points as your plan is being implemented.

DECISION POINTS

1. **Do we need to adjust the "mix" of resources?** (Refer back to your budget on page 75, and your list of mini-resources in the chart on page 49.)

2. **Will it take more resources to do this at all?**

3. **Should we try another strategy or modify this one?** Look back at your brainstorming of alternate strategies on page 39.)

4. **Should we drop the plan altogether?** (What are my criteria for making a go/no-go decision? Should we drop the plan if it's only 50% effective? 30%? 10%?

WHEN TO DECIDE?

1.

2.

3.

4.

STEP 5

B

Look at each part of the plan and anticipate where a **comparison** of actual performance and planned performance might yield information that will help make key decisions.

What could go wrong?

Usually we think of making decisions like these only when something goes wrong. In fact, when things are going right, we often make the implicit decision *not* to make any changes. In either case, whether things are going well or badly, we need to know where to look for information that will help us make an informed decision.

Your plan—resources, activities, strategy, and objective—gives you a series of places to look for information, so you can compare what actually happens with what you expected would happen. Are the **resources** being used successfully to produce activities? Are the **activities** successfully resulting in the strategy being carried out? Is the **strategy** (or strategies) making it possible for you to reach the objective? To what extent is the **objective** being met?

"So now you have this well-thought-out plan!"

As shown before on page 83, if the plan is working smoothly, resources are producing activities, which add up to a strategy, which results in the objective being met.*

If you find that the objective isn't being met, you will want to go back and look at resources, activities, and strategy to find the source of the difficulty.

The obstacle may lie with the **resources** (not enough time spent, wrong people assigned). If so, the result will be that the activities won't be completed. (Task force doesn't meet.) Therefore, the strategy won't work, and the objective won't be met.

The obstacle may lie with the **activities.** (Staff approach to employee/advocate groups is too superficial or too authoritarian.) If so, the result will be that the strategy won't work. (Representatives don't agree to serve on the task force.) Therefore, the objective won't be met.

Finally, the obstacle may lie with the **strategy**. (Even though the task force develops the Affirmative Action Plan, it still isn't accepted by employee/advocate groups.) Therefore, the result will also be that the objective isn't met.

*The concept illustrated here is adapted from Carol H. Weiss, *Evaluation Research,* © 1972, p. 38. Adapted by permission of Prentice-Hall, Inc., Englewood Cliffs, New Jersey.

STEP 5
B

When you plan, you make assumptions about the world and the future. Once you begin to act in that world and the future becomes now, you may have to revise your assumptions. New opportunities may be available, or new problems may have arisen. From this you can see that evaluation is a way of checking on the accuracy of the assumptions you made in planning.

RESOURCES You assumed that specified *resources* would be needed and available for certain activities. How does this assumption hold up? Are more or less resources needed? Different kinds of resources? Different combinations of resources?

ACTIVITIES Also, you assumed that specified *activities* would result in completion of a certain strategy. Was that assumption faulty? Would different activities be more effective? Do you need fewer activities? More activities?

STRATEGY You also assumed that the *strategy* would help achieve the objective. Was this assumption incorrect? Can the strategy be modified? Or was it a bad idea to start with? Was more than one strategy needed?

OBJECTIVE Finally, you assumed the *objective* was a good one for you to pursue. Was this a good assumption? Or was the objective too ambitious? Inappropriate? Do you have new information that suggests other objectives?

These examples illustrate how the different levels of the plan can be used continually as a source of evaluation questions. Depending on the answers to these questions, decisions can be made that alter the plan to keep it on target. By anticipating troubles now, you can prepare yourself to look for danger signals and avoid problems before they occur.

There is space on the next page for you to use to identify possible points where your plan might break down. List questions you may want to ask about your resources, activities, strategy, and objectives as a way of anticipating modifications you may need to make. Use the questions suggested above to get you started.

What could go wrong?

Resources:

Activities:

Strategy:

Objective:

STEP 5
C

Design *measures* of appropriateness, adequacy, effectiveness,
efficiency, and side effects in
order to compare actual and
planned performance.*

Measures
to Evaluate Each
Question

So far, you have anticipated the decisions that might need to be made about
the plan and have seen where you might want to compare planned and actual
performance. Now, you can get down to the business of designing *measures* that
will give you the information you need to make *comparisons* in order to make
good *decisions.*

To do this, let's return to the five basic evaluative criteria used in Step 3
(pp. 50–51) in considering which strategy to implement. Looking at these criteria
again, you'll see that they can be applied *at any time* in the planning or implementation process and at any level (resources, activities, strategy, and
objective).

Here is a review of the general questions asked for evaluative criteria at the
various levels:

1. *Appropriateness*—Is it "right" for you to use these resources, to do these
   activities and strategies, and to strive for this objective? This is basically
   a value question that asks whether "most people" would agree that it's
   okay to do these things.

2. *Adequacy*—Are these resources "enough" to carry out the activities? Are
   you doing "enough" activities to pull off the strategy? Is the strategy
   "sufficient" to accomplish the objective? Is the objective "big enough"
   given the size of the problem?

"You design the measure only after you know what it is you want to measure."

3. **Effectiveness**—To what extent have the actual use of resources, carrying out of activities and strategies, and meeting of objectives happened as planned? Have you used all the **resources** you'd planned to, and do they combine to produce the planned activities? Have you done all the planned **activities,** and do they result in a completed strategy? Was the planned **strategy** carried out, and has it resulted in the objective being met? To what extent has the **objective** been met and the problem reduced?

4. **Efficiency**—Could the **resources** be combined differently or different resources used so that the same activities could be produced at lower costs? Could the **activity** process be changed so that the same activities could be produced at a lower cost? How costly is the **strategy** compared to the benefits obtained? Would another strategy accomplish the same objective at lower cost? How does the actual cost per unit of **objective** achieved compare with the planned cost per unit of planned objective?

5. **Side effects**—What are the good and bad, anticipated and unanticipated side effects of the resources, activities, strategy, and objective? To what extent did the anticipated side effects occur? What unanticipated side effects occurred?

*These evaluative criteria are adapted from a paper by Professor O. Lynn Deniston, "Evaluation of Disease Control Programs," Washington, D.C., U.S. Department of Health, Education, and Welfare, Public Health Service, March, 1972.

STEP 5
C

The format illustrated below can be used to identify which type of evaluation question you might want to ask at one particular time. It would be helpful to have a measure that can give you the answer to each of these questions. For example, if you find after three months that there has been no impact on your problem situation, you might suspect that something is wrong with the resources used. Using this chart as a guide, you would look at measures of how appropriate, adequate, effective, and efficient your use of resources has been and whether there have been any unanticipated side effects that may be blocking the process.

Evaluative Questions	Levels of Plan	RESOURCES	ACTIVITIES Tasks/Activities	STRATEGY (or STRATEGIES)	OBJECTIVE
Appropriateness					
Adequacy					
Effectiveness					
Efficiency					
Side Effects					

So far, we have talked about what we want to measure without saying what we mean by "measure." A measure may be as precise as "the number of dropouts who return to school" or as vague as "employees are more or less involved in decision-making."

Measures to Evaluate Each Question

> **A MEASURE is:**
>
> The amount of something that exists at a certain time.

An important principle of measurement is that you design the measure *after* you know what it is that you want to measure. That is, you first need to think about what decisions you will be making and what information you will need to make those decisions before you decide what to measure. It is far too easy to count something just because it's countable. The only trouble is you may be wasting a lot of everyone's time and coming up with worthless information.

This leads to the next principle: it's best to be stingy about what you measure, to measure *only* those things that will give you the critical information you need. For some information, you may want to measure continuously (every day, week, or month). You may want to take other measures intermittently (every six months or every year or when a crisis occurs).

It is painfully obvious that the state-of-the-art of measurement in the social and organizational sciences is rather primitive. In most cases, there simply are no "perfect" measures that will tell you exactly what you want to know. The best you can do is pick an indicator, something that seems to come close to the information you are after. However, once you have picked a measure and said you are going to use it to indicate the degree of success or failure, you have to agree to stick by it. It's not fair to decide—after a measurement points to failure—that it was really a lousy measure after all!

With these points in mind, and using the sample measures on the next page as a guide, practice designing a few measures of appropriateness, adequacy, effectiveness, efficiency, and side effects for the various levels of your plan. Again, the easiest way to do this is to ask: "How will I know whether this resource, this activity, this strategy, or this objective meets the five evaluative criteria?" The answer is a ***measure***.

The sample on the next page is provided to illustrate the kind of measurement possible, not to suggest that you will necessarily need all of these measures for any one evaluation design. Use the grid to help you decide which measures will provide the information you will need to evaluate ***your*** plan. Again. remember to measure only what you need. (Measures in boldface are the ones that will be used later in illustrating sources of data.)

Sample
Measures to Evaluate Each Question

Evaluative Questions / Levels of Plan	RESOURCES (Personnel manager working ¼ time on this project)	ACTIVITY (Obtaining commitment of group representatives to serve on task force)	STRATEGY (Task force of employee advocates to develop plan)	OBJECTIVE (Affirmative Action Plan that has the support of employee advocate groups)
Appropriateness	Number of people who agree it is reasonable to assign the personnel manager to this type of project	Number of people who agree it's all right for management to ask for such participation	**Number of people who agree it's acceptable for a plan to be developed by such a group**	Number of people who agree it makes sense for such a plan to be endorsed by affected parties
Adequacy	**Number of staff hours spent to carry out the activity of obtaining commitment**	Number of key groups represented on the task force	Number of groups endorsing the plan	Number of groups endorsing the plan compared to number potentially having an interest in the plan
Effectiveness	Number of staff hours devoted to this activity compared to planned number	Number of groups represented compared to planned number	Number of groups endorsing the plan compared to planned number	**Extent that formal endorsement means actual support of the plan (Number of grievances filed, informal reports of employee dissatisfaction)**
Efficiency	Cost per representative contacted compared to planned cost	Cost per group endorsing plan compared to planned cost	**Cost per group endorsing the plan compared to cost per group if plan had been developed by personnel manager and sent to groups for comment**	Cost per group actually supporting the plan compared to planned cost
Side Effects	Number of employee grievances delayed because personnel manager was tied up with this project (negative)	**Number of new employee ideas obtained, problems uncovered in process of contacting representatives (positive/negative)**	Number of times this approach used in solving other organizational problems (positive) / Number of hours spent by everyone in organizational decision-making instead of maintaining water system (negative)	Number of other issues where management receives employee support because of improved morale generated by this process (positive)

Measures to Evaluate Each Question

Evaluative Questions / Levels of Plan	OBJECTIVE	STRATEGY	ACTIVITIES (Including tasks and activities)	RESOURCES
Appropriateness				
Adequacy				
Effectiveness				
Efficiency				
Side Effects				

STEP 5

D

Figure out how to obtain the data for these measurements.

Data Sources

Now that you have designed some measures, you can begin to think about how to obtain the data you need.

DATA are:

The numbers you get when you take the measure.

The *measure* is:
"The number of secretaries who have improved their shorthand skills."

One piece of *data* might be:
"Fifty secretaries have improved their shorthand skills."

We analyze this data and arrive at the *information* that:
"This strategy is 50% effective in meeting the objective that 100 secretaries improve their shorthand skills."

Chances are you will be asking evaluative questions that have never been asked before, so you will need to find new ways of collecting the data. Maybe some of the data are already being gathered, but you need to get them from someone else's records. Maybe you will need to design new or revised forms for your own organization, or you may need to ask someone else to gather data for you.

"It is far too easy to count something just because it is countable..."

It is important to keep this process as simple and unobtrusive as possible. No one wants another form to fill out. Maybe in the process of collecting this data you will find that you're collecting other information that isn't needed, and you will be able to *eliminate* some unnecessary paperwork that is currently being done.

Here is a list of some familiar ways to collect data:

- Interviews
- Questionnaires
- Observation
- Ratings (by peers, staff, experts)
- Tests of attitudes, values, personality, preferences, norms, beliefs
- Institutional records and reports
- Projective tests
- Clinical examinations
- Financial records
- Documents (minutes of board meetings, newspaper accounts, transcripts of trials)
- Tests of information, interpretation skills, use of knowledge
- Government statistics

The chart on the next page illustrates a format for identifying the sources you will use to collect data for your measures. (Measures are those shown in boldface in the chart on page 98.)

Sample Data Sources

MEASURE	SOURCE OF DATA
Number of people who agree it's acceptable for a plan to be developed by such a group (Measure of **appropriateness** of **strategy**)	Show of hands at a staff meeting
Number of staff hours spent to carry out the activity of obtaining commitment (Measure of **adequacy** of **resources**)	Time records of personnel manager and clerical assistant
Extent that formal endorsement means actual support of the plan (Measure of **effectiveness** of **objective**)	Number of grievances filed about the plan Reports of employee dissatisfaction received formally or informally by department director or personnel manager (A mechanism for recording these informat reports will be needed, e.g. a logbook kept by personnel manager.) Newspaper articles Articles in union newsletter
Cost per group endorsing the plan compared to cost per group if plan had been developed by personnel manager and sent to groups for comment (Measure of **efficiency** of **strategy**)	Calculation of hours and/or dollars spent (from time record of staff x hourly salary) divided by number of groups endorsing the plan; comparison of this figure with estimated cost using another strategy
Number of new employee ideas obtained, problems uncovered in the process of contacting representatives (Measure of **side effects** of **activity**)	From personnel manager's daily log recording comments received, and from feedback to department director from sources inside and outside the organization (If data are recorded systematically, the chances of action on the comments *may* be increased!)

Data Sources

In the space below, list some possible ways you can collect data for each of the measures you have designed. (Look back at your chart on page 99.)

MEASURE	SOURCE OF DATA

Determine who will *analyze* the data, how, and when.

Data Gathering & Analysis

At this stage you know what *decisions* may need to be made with the evaluation information. You know what parts of the plan have to be looked at and *compared* with actual performance. You've planned a way of *measuring* various aspects of the plan to produce the information you need and figured out where the *data* will come from. Now, what will you do with all this data?

The answer to this will, of course, depend on the size, complexity, and nature of your plan. At the simplest, data analysis may be a staff member reviewing the records, drawing conclusions, and reporting verbally to other staff. At its most complex, data analysis may involve elaborate computer processing that results in a multi-volume research study on a large-scale, comprehensive plan.

Basically, though, there are just a few things to think about in designing this phase of the evaluation process:

1. Who is going to collect the data and analyze it?

2. How should this analysis be done?

3. When should the analysis be done?

STEP 5

E

Sample
Data Gathering
& Analysis

1. **Who will collect and analyze the data?**
   The personnel manager is the staff member responsible for the plan. He will also collect and analyze the data.

2. **How will the analysis be done?**
   Since this is a relatively simple plan, no elaborate technology, such as data processing, will be necessary. Most of the data will be from the personnel manager's personal experience in implementing the plan. From his own records of time spent, people contacted, and commitments made, he will simply make the necessary comparisons with the plan and draw his conclusions from these comparisons.

3. **When will the analysis take place?**
   He will evaluate the use of resources and activity process after the first month and at monthly intervals. He will report this to the department director, who will evaluate the strategy and its impact on objectives after the first month and after three months.

Data Gathering
& Analysis

In the space below, jot down some ideas about how the data gathering and analysis phase of the evaluation might be done with your plan.

1. **Who will collect and analyze the data?**

2. **How will the analysis be done?**

3. **When will the analysis take place?**

USING EVALUATIVE INFORMATION

STEP 6

In the last chapter, you identified decision points where evaluative information would be needed and designed a process for obtaining that information. Next you will consider how to use that information to make individual and organizational decisions to keep the plan going or make needed modifications. This step concerns the process by which the plan or program become "institutionalized" as part of the ongoing life of the organization. In this step, it will be important to think of feedback being used in different ways—by managers and boards to make administrative and policy decisions and by staff members to make day-to-day operational decisions. At both levels, there are at least two steps to making sure that evaluative feedback is used. The third step will complete the evaluation design.

A Present the information in a way that increases the possibility of acceptance.

B Make sure the right information gets to the right people at the right time.

C Summarize how you will use evaluative information about your plan in the organization.

This part of the planning/evaluation process requires using information from many of the preceding steps. If you have planned carefully, involved the right people, and designed the evaluation well, the chances are increased that your organization will have the information it needs at the right time and place and will be prepared to accept and use the information.

Evaluative information may be (and most often is) presented informally and verbally—a supervisor's feedback on a staff member's performance, an employee review of a colleague's paper, a status report to a policy-making board. Or the information may be presented formally and in writing—an employee's annual performance appraisal, a written critique of an in-house report, or an in-depth evaluative research report.

The examples and exercises that follow focus on negative feedback because it is frequently the most difficult to give and to receive. However, positive feedback is not always easy either, and its importance is too often overlooked. Given to those involved in implementing a plan, positive feedback is an intrinsic reward, a source of ongoing motivation. Given to outsiders, such as a board of directors or a community group, positive feedback on a plan's success increases everyone's feeling of pride and accomplishment. We can all use more positive feedback. Practice with a friend, spouse, or co-worker!

STEP 6

A

Present the information in a way that increases the possibility of acceptance.

Written & Verbal Feedback

Here are a number of ideas for getting a positive response to your plan.*

1. Use existing channels of communication and decision making in the organization, both formal and informal. For example: reports at staff meetings; feedback at regular employee evaluation sessions.

2. Build in incentives and rewards for using the information. For example, using Management by Objectives (MBO), an organization's internal reward system may be based on meeting agreed-upon objectives.

3. Present useful comparisons. If one strategy isn't working, present information about *feasible* alternatives.

4. Be nondefensive about the information. Treat it as an indication of success or possible trouble, not as gospel.

5. Submit the report in a form and language that the decision makers can understand. Board members may reject a proposal if it's written in professional jargon that does not make sense to them.

*From Carol H. Weiss, *Evaluation Research,* © 1972, pp. 117–121. Adapted by permission of Prentice-Hall, Inc., Englewood Cliffs, New Jersey.

"...think of feedback being used
in different ways."

To prepare for presenting evaluative feedback in your organization, try this exercise on giving verbal feedback. Imagine that you have obtained some information through your evaluative process that indicates certain behaviors or actions of a colleague or subordinate are hampering the implementation of your plan. Write a brief dialogue between yourself and the other person, with you giving the feedback in a way that would encourage the other person to change his or her behavior.

EXERCISE ON VERBAL FEEDBACK

1. **What is the problem?**

2. **Who is the person?**

3. **What would you say first?**

4. **How would the other person respond?**

5. **What would you say next?**

6. **How might the person conclude the conversation?**

Use the tips for giving and receiving feedback on the following page to evaluate your dialogue. Make changes as appropriate to increase your chances for success.

STEP 6

Below are a few hints for giving feedback to increase the chances of its being accepted and for receiving feedback nondefensively without feeling personally attacked.*

1. Focus feedback on descriptions of behavior, rather than on judgments about personality.

   DON'T SAY: "John, you idiot, you have tried to blackmail people into joining the task force."

   SAY INSTEAD: "John, several people have told me that you suggested they would be sorry if they didn't join the task force."

2. Give feedback on a specific situation, preferably soon after it has occurred, rather than giving feedback on general behavior that has happened over a long period of time.

   DON'T SAY: "For the past three months, John, you have tried to railroad your ideas through and haven't listened to anyone else on this task force."

   SAY INSTEAD: "Sarah made a good suggestion there, John. You ignored it. Perhaps we should discus it further, rather than moving on just yet."

3. Focus feedback on sharing information and exploring alternatives, rather than on giving advice and offering solutions.

   DON'T SAY: "John, a lot of people are complaining about meetings not starting on time. You should make a point of opening the meeting right at nine o'clock."

   SAY INSTEAD: "A number of task force members have complained that meetings never start on time. Is that because you're waiting for everyone to arrive? Is there something you can do to satisfy the complaint? How about contracting with everyone to show up on time or suggesting a more convenient time? What ideas do you have?"

Notice that putting suggestions in a positive way makes it much easier for John to respond.

*Adapted from a paper by George F. J. Lehner, Professor of Psychology, University of California, Los Angeles. Used with permission.

Now try the following exercise on providing written feedback. Imagine that you have obtained some concrete, factual information about the implementation of your plan that indicates change in strategy may be necessary. Write a memo to your supervisor in which you present the evaluative information as evidence to support your recommended course of action.

EXERCISE ON WRITTEN FEEDBACK

TO:

FROM:

RE:

STEP 6
B

Make sure the right information gets to the right people at the right time.*

Who needs what information when?

We don't often think about the information on which decisions are based, but obviously different people need different types and amounts of information depending on their roles in the organization and the kind of decisions they make. A staff member needs detailed feedback about day-to-day performance. A supervisor needs information to compare the effectiveness of different approaches. A manager is more interested in impact and cost effectiveness. The board of directors needs to know about long-term directions and community reactions. Timing is also important. The best information in the world is useless if it's submitted after a major decision has already been made.

*From Carol H. Weiss, *Evaluation Research,* © 1972, pp. 117–121. Adapted by permission of Prentice-Hall, Inc., Englewood Cliffs, New Jersey.

"The best information in the world is useless if it is submitted after a major decision has already been made."

Using our familiar example, the chart on the following page illustrates how you might prepare in advance to make sure the right people get the right information at the right time. To begin filling in this chart, the personnel manager looked back at decision points identified on page 88 and located three that represented the different organizational levels. Then he identified who would be making each decision, what information the decision maker would need, and when the information would be needed.

A blank chart is provided for you to plan how to use evaluative information in your organization. Choose a sample decision or action from three levels of your organization (operational, administrative, and policy) to give you a feel for the different information requirements of different organization members. Charts on pages 89 and 93 will help refresh your memory on key decision points in your strategy.

STEP 6
B

Sample
Who needs
what information when?

Organization Level	Sample Decision or Action	Who Makes Decision?	What Information Is Needed by Decision Maker?	When Is Information Needed by Decision Maker?
Operational	Would potential task force members respond more positively if they were approached differently?	Personnel manager	Verbal feedback about his style or manner in approaching potential task force members	As soon as possible after someone (supervisor, peer, supporter) observes the negative effect of his style or manner
Administrative	Should there be a three-month extension for completing the Affirmative Action Plan?	Department director	Indication from employees and community groups that more time would result in more support	One month before original July 1 deadline
Policy	Should the strategy be changed to develop an Affirmative Action Plan without a representative task force?	Department director	Time being spent on the project (too much); conflict within the organization (too much)	With three-month evaluation report

Who needs what information when?

Organization Level	Sample Decision or Action	Who Makes Decision?	What Information Is Needed by Decision Maker?	When Is Information Needed by Decision Maker?
Operational				
Administrative				
Policy				

Summarize how you will use evaluative information about your plan in the organization.

Sample
Reporting of
Evaluative Feedback

As the final stage in designing your evaluation process, describe how the information produced in your evaluative design from Step 5 will be used. Below is a sample chart. Use the worksheet on the following page to summarize what information will be needed, by whom, and in what format.

Person(s) Receiving Information	Type of Information	Time of Report	Format of Report
Feedback to operating staff (personnel manager)	Resources used (personal) Activity process (day-to-day) Completed activities Schedule followed?	Weekly	Verbal feedback from department director; information received from inside and outside organization Feedback to personnel manager from his own experiences
Feedback to administrators (department director)	Resources used (overall program) Activity process (general overview) Schedule followed?	Weekly	Written report (memo) from personnel manager
Feedback to policy makers (department director)	Strategy successful? Progress toward objective	After 3 months and 6 months	Formal progress report suitable for distribution to other departments and mayor

Person(s) Receiving Information	Type of Information	Time of Report	Format of Report
Feedback to operating staff			
Feedback to administrators			
Feedback to policy makers			

THE NEXT STEP

In planning, the end is but the beginning—a time to start implementing the planned strategy and begin the continual process of evaluating "where we are and where we're going." Frequently this process means a return to the drawing board—going back and rethinking part of the planning process. At the best, you'll be refining your time schedule (speeding up or extending the deadline as the inevitable delays creep in) or detailing the tasks planned for a given activity. At the worst, you'll be going back and redefining the problem or designing a whole new strategy.

At some point, it's a good idea to step outside the entire process and look at the plan with as much objectivity as you can muster to ask yourself if the whole thing has been worth doing at all. (This is very hard to do; but if you don't, it may be done by outsiders with painful results for you!)

"The end is but the beginning..."

After you've been involved with the plan for six months or a year, pull back from it, sit down, and ask yourself:

- Was it really worth it?

- What did all this effort amount to?

- What have we really accomplished?

- Have we made any impact on the original problem?

- Was it really a problem after all?

This kind of soul searching is a change in perspective from the nitty-gritty analysis you've been doing. But it's easy to become so wrapped up in the details of planning that you forget why you were doing all this in the first place. So—set aside time every now and then to look at the big picture and assess the overall impact of what you are doing. Keep this final planning idea handy in your hip pocket!

EPILOGUE

INITIATING ORGANIZATIONAL CHANGE

HIP POCKET GUIDE

TO PLANNING & EVALUATION

Planning on paper—as you've done in this workbook—is one thing. It's quite another to actually implement a plan within an organization. Introducing any new plan is likely to mean that something will have to change—from the routines of an individual to the functioning of the entire organization—and change, for most of us, is not always easy to handle. As a planner trying to behave rationally, you may be suddenly cast in the role of an organizational change agent and may find yourself tilting at windmills you never knew existed. Because of this, it's important to touch briefly on the vast subject of organizational change, although it is really beyond the scope of the **Hip Pocket Guide.** This section includes some ideas to help you think about the overall problem of introducing your carefully designed plan into your organization.

The steps you might follow in thinking about this are:

Analyze your organization's capacity for change and your own attitudes toward change.

Think about the process of change as it typically occurs in organizations.

Based on the analysis of your own organization's capacity for change and the organizational change process, anticipate what problems you might encounter in introducing your plan.

Prepare your strategy for getting your plan accepted in your organization.

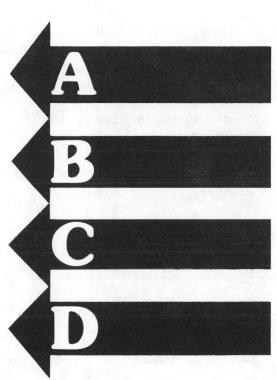

In this section, you'll find some basic theoretical background material on change in organizations along with exercises and guidelines to help you in your change efforts.

EPILOGUE A

Change!

At this point you'll have a chance to assess your own beliefs about change and your own typical responses to change. Following are two checklists for you to use to measure your personal "change quotient."*

BELIEFS ABOUT CHANGE

Check whether you believe the following statements are true, sometimes true, or false. In the space provided under each statement expand upon why you responded as you did.

True	Sometimes True	False		
☐	☐	☐	1.	People tend to resist change.
☐	☐	☐	2.	Only large or momentous changes are worthwhile.
☐	☐	☐	3.	Nothing can be changed overnight.
☐	☐	☐	4.	Change means improvement.
☐	☐	☐	5.	Change brings hardships for some.
☐	☐	☐	6.	Change brings reward for the instigators.
☐	☐	☐	7.	No change is possible in a bureaucracy.
☐	☐	☐	8.	Technological change should be slowed.
☐	☐	☐	9.	Change usually comes by chance.
☐	☐	☐	10.	People can adapt to any change.

This exercise will get you thinking about how you feel about change and your role in instigating and implementing change. You might discuss your attitudes about change with a co-worker or your supervisor, or you might notice how your approach to planning and implementing strategies is colored by your attitudes toward change.

   If you answered "True" to questions 2, 4, 6, and 10, it may indicate a need to be a little more realistic. If you answered "True" to questions 7 and 9, this may indicate a pessimistic attitude that may make it hard for you to work energetically for change. If you answered "True" to questions 1, 3, and 5, it indicates a recognition of the real problems involved in change.

"You... may find yourself tilting at windmills you never knew existed!"

YOUR CHANGE QUOTIENT

Answer "yes" or "no" to these questions. (You may also want to consider how these questions apply to your supervisor, peers, and subordinates; or you may want to have other staff members rate you with this checklist to see how their ratings compare with your self-rating.)

Yes	No		
☐	☐	1.	Can you get enthusiastic about problems outside your specialized area?
☐	☐	2.	Do you feel the excitement and challenge of finding a solution to problems in many areas, regardless of whether they are major or minor challenges?
☐	☐	3.	When a problem seems to hold little or no interest, do you nevertheless try to develop an interest in the problem's possibilities?
☐	☐	4.	Do you know what is expected of you by management?
☐	☐	5.	Do you seldom assume limitations and lack of freedom in your work?
☐	☐	6.	Do you sometimes set the problem aside temporarily to get a new perspective, without closing your mind to it or giving up?
☐	☐	7.	Do you resist "blocking" a project even though you think it trivial and distracting from problems more to your taste?
☐	☐	8.	Do you accept the occasional illogic of your mind, recognizing that it can lead you to solutions in managing change?
☐	☐	9.	Do you commonly carry a notebook to put stray ideas in writing?
☐	☐	10.	Do you seek many ideas, rather than becoming satisfied with one or a few?
☐	☐	11.	Do you know how to simplify and organize your impressions?

Your quotient is high if you answered "Yes" to at least eight of the eleven questions. Innovators of change need great tenacity of purpose and stubborn resistance to discouragement. They need initiative, curiosity, and the ability to simplify the many reactions and events that occur during a change process.

*Adapted from *Managing Change: The Strategies of Making Change Work for You,* by John S. Morgan. Copyright © 1972 by McGraw-Hill, Inc. Used with permission of McGraw-Hill Book Company. Questionnaire format designed by Celeste Sturdevant.

EPILOGUE A

Change!

Some organizations are more open and receptive to change than others. The organizational diagnosis on the opposite page may help you assess your organization's general operating style and what potential blocks to change you might run into. For each question, circle the answer that best fits your organization. You may also want to get your supervisor, your co-workers, and your subordinates to try this exercise so that you can compare your perceptions of the organization with theirs. Their ideas may help you determine the best approaches to change in your organization. A good approach in one organization may be totally inappropriate in another. Here are example change strategies appropriate to each of the four types of organizations shown:

➡ **System 1**—You'd better make your boss think the new idea is his own. Starting from the bottom up will only ensure failure.

➡ **System 2**—You will need to spend time thoroughly selling new ideas to your boss.

➡ **System 3**—Your boss expects you to consult with her before acting.

➡ **System 4**—You will need to get inputs in the early stages of a project from all levels of the organization.

*The Characteristics of Management Systems chart on the facing page is an adaptation of the Profile of Organizational Characteristics from *The Human Organization* by Rensis Likert. Copyright © 1967 by McGraw-Hill, Inc. Used with permission of McGraw-Hill Book Company.

Characteristics of Management Systems*

	Type of Organization Organizational Factors	SYSTEM 1 Authoritative/ Exploitive	SYSTEM 2 Authoritative/ Benevolent	SYSTEM 3 Consultative	SYSTEM 4 Participative
LEADERSHIP	1. How much confidence is shown in subordinates?	None	Condescending	Substantial	Complete
	2. How free do they feel to talk to superiors about job?	Not at all	Not very	Rather free	Fully free
	3. Are subordinates' ideas sought and used, if worthy?	Seldom	Sometimes	Usually	Always
MOTIVATION	4. Is predominant use made of: (1) fear, (2) threats, (3) punishment, (4) rewards, (5) involvement?	1, 2, 3, occasionally 4	4, some 3	4, some 3 and 5	5, 4 based on group-set goals
	5. Where is responsibility felt for achieving organization's goals?	Mostly at top	Top and middle	Fairly general	At all levels
COMMUNICATION	6. How much communication is aimed at achieving organization's objectives?	Very little	Little	Quite a bit	A great deal
	7. What is the direction of information flow?	Downward	Downward mostly	Down and up	Down, up, and sideways
	8. How is downward communication accepted?	With suspicion	Possibly with suspicion	With caution	With an open mind
	9. How accurate is upward communication?	Often wrong	Censored for the boss	Limited accuracy	Accurate
	10. How well do superiors know problems faced by subordinates?	Know little	Some knowledge	Quite well	Very well
DECISIONS	11. At what level are decisions formally made?	Mostly at top	Policy at top, some delegation	Broad policy at top, more delegation	Throughout, but well integrated
	12. What is the origin of technical and professional knowledge used in decision making?	Top management	Upper and middle	To a certain extent throughout	To a great extent throughout
	13. Are subordinates involved in decisions related to their work?	Not at all	Occasionally consulted	Generally consulted	Fully consulted
	14. What does decision-making process contribute to motivation?	Nothing, often weakens it	Relatively little	Some contribution	Substantial contribution
GOALS	15. How are organizational goals established?	Orders issued	Orders, some comment invited	After discussion, by orders	By group action (except in crisis)
	16. How much covert resistance to goals is present?	Strong resistance	Moderate resistance	Some resistance at times	Little or none
CONTROL	17. How concentrated are review and control functions?	Highly at top	Relatively highly at top	Moderate delegation to lower levels	Quite widely shared
	18. Is there an informal organization resisting the formal one?	Yes	Usually	Sometimes	No, same goals as formal
	19. What are cost, productivity, and other control data used for?	Policing, punishing	Reward and punishment	Reward, some self-guidance	Self-guidance, problem solving

EPILOGUE B

The Change Process

One way to visualize the process of change in an organization is to imagine an ice cube melting, turning into water, and then being frozen again into ice. In organizational terms, the process can be seen as three stages: "unfreezing" the existing status quo, "changing" through some set of actions, and "refreezing" into a new stable pattern.*

*Adapted from a conceptualization originally published by Kurt Lewin in *Human Relations*, Vol. 1, No. 1, 1947. Used with permission of Plenum Publishing Corp., New York. The concept has been developed further by Ronald Lippitt, et al. in *The Dynamics of Planned Change.* New York: Harcourt, Brace & World, 1958.

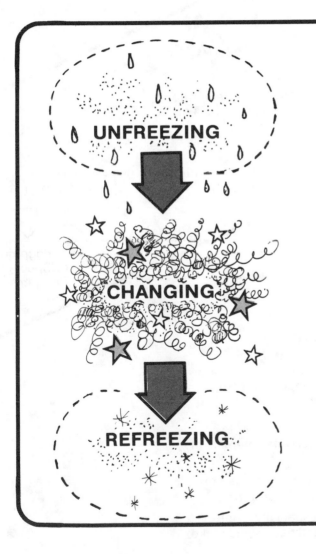

Change may be initiated by a crisis in the organization, new demands placed on the organization, or innovation proposed by someone in the organization. The old ways are opened to questions, and the climate for change exists.

Change occurs through a random process of looking for new solutions, or a planned approach to solving a problem. There is uncertainty, searching, and probably conflict.

Change is institutionalized as the new innovation becomes the new "standard operating procedure."

EPILOGUE
B

A more complex way of illustrating the dynamics of successful organizational change is shown below. This diagram shows how change, beginning as pressure on top management, can set off a series of reactions ending with the acceptance of new practices if the process is guided well. It also shows a way to work with directives to you to make changes in a "top-down" organization.*

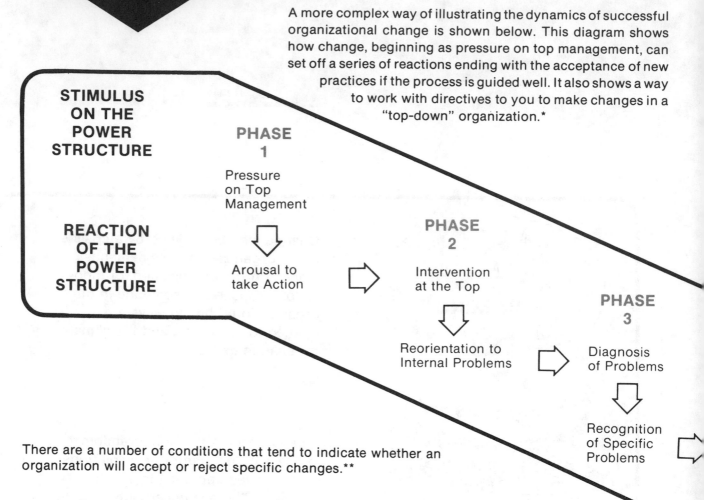

STIMULUS ON THE POWER STRUCTURE

REACTION OF THE POWER STRUCTURE

PHASE 1

Pressure on Top Management

⇩

Arousal to take Action

⇨

PHASE 2

Intervention at the Top

⇩

Reorientation to Internal Problems

⇨

PHASE 3

Diagnosis of Problems

⇩

Recognition of Specific Problems

⇨

There are a number of conditions that tend to indicate whether an organization will accept or reject specific changes.**

CONDITIONS FOR ACCEPTING AND SUPPORTING CHANGE

1. When the change will contribute to reaching an important goal, when the individual identifies with the organizational goal

2. When there is dissatisfaction with the status quo

3. When the change will further the professional or personal interests of the individual

4. When the change seems "right" because it fits the way things are usually done or when the logic of the situation is overpowering

5. When the change reflects the group's thinking, especially where conformity seems important or where the individual has helped make a decision and feels obliged to support it

6. When the change involves small changes in behavior that are actively reinforced

The Change Process

CONDITIONS FOR REJECTING AND RESISTING CHANGE

1. When the change endangers organizational goals or security (and the individual identifies with the organization)

2. When the change would endanger the individual's sense of personal security

3. When the change would violate what the individual feels is an important standard of behavior or performance

4. When the change seems illogical

5. When the change is contrary to what the group thinks should be done

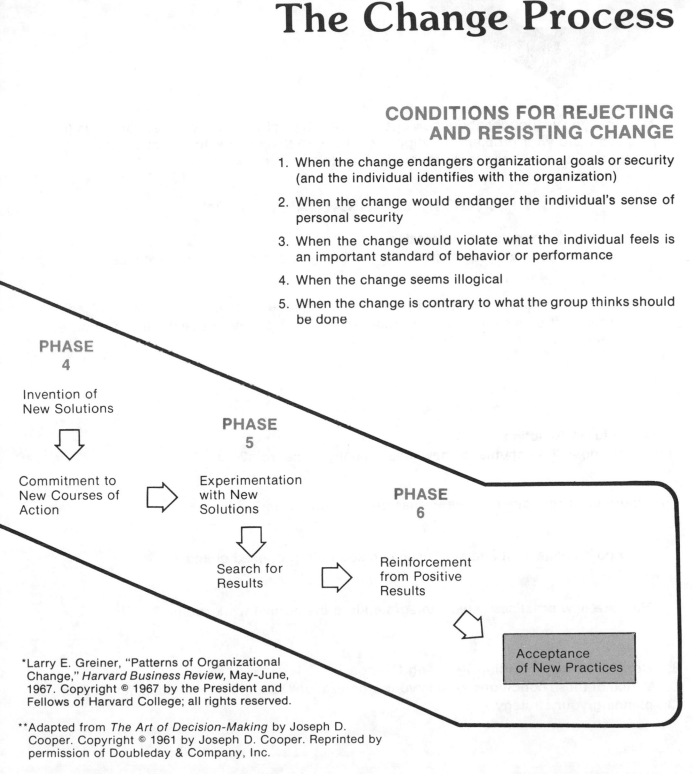

PHASE 4

Invention of New Solutions

⇩

Commitment to New Courses of Action

⇨

PHASE 5

Experimentation with New Solutions

⇩

Search for Results

⇨

PHASE 6

Reinforcement from Positive Results

⇩

Acceptance of New Practices

*Larry E. Greiner, "Patterns of Organizational Change," *Harvard Business Review,* May–June, 1967. Copyright © 1967 by the President and Fellows of Harvard College; all rights reserved.

**Adapted from *The Art of Decision-Making* by Joseph D. Cooper. Copyright © 1961 by Joseph D. Cooper. Reprinted by permission of Doubleday & Company, Inc.

EPILOGUE
B

Now that you've thought about how change might typically occur, consider your specific organization and your problem situation. Use the worksheet below to reflect on how your organization fits in with the three theoretical models presented.

CHANGE IN YOUR ORGANIZATION

1. **Unfreezing ➡ Changing ➡ Refreezing**
   Can you characterize your organization as being in one of these three stages?

   How will this affect the success of your planned change? (For example, if your organization has just experienced a major reorganization, this may not be the time for more innovation.)

2. **Stimulus ➡ Reaction**
   Where does the impetus for new ideas usually come from?

   Where does resistance for new ideas usually come from?

   How do management and staff usually respond to proposed changes?

   How are new practices usually integrated into the normal work routine?

3. **Conditions for Accepting/Resisting Change**
   Which of these conditions exist in your organization? (Don't forget to consider them in planning your strategy.)

Based on the analysis of your own organization's capacity for change and the organizational change process, anticipate what problems you might encounter in introducing your plan.

EPILOGUE C

Reactions to Change

Personal attitudes toward change may produce a number of collective reactions to a given innovation. Group reactions may range along the following scale:

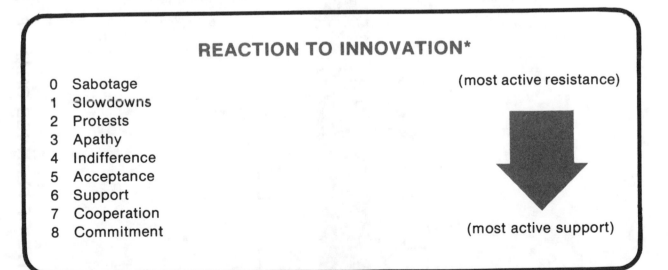

REACTION TO INNOVATION*

0 Sabotage
1 Slowdowns
2 Protests
3 Apathy
4 Indifference
5 Acceptance
6 Support
7 Cooperation
8 Commitment

(most active resistance)

(most active support)

How is your organization likely to react to *your* planned change? Use the force-field analysis you completed in Step 3 (p. 43). Check those helping and hindering forces that pertain to internal organization responses as well as those external forces that affect organizational responses directly.

*Adapted from *Managerial Effectiveness* by William J. Reddin. Copyright © 1970 by McGraw-Hill, Inc. Used with permission of McGraw-Hill Book Company.

EPILOGUE C

Now fill in the force-field analysis below with these forces and any additional factors that you can think of.* (The force-field analysis diagram has been altered slightly to illustrate another variation of this technique.)

FORCE-FIELD ANALYSIS

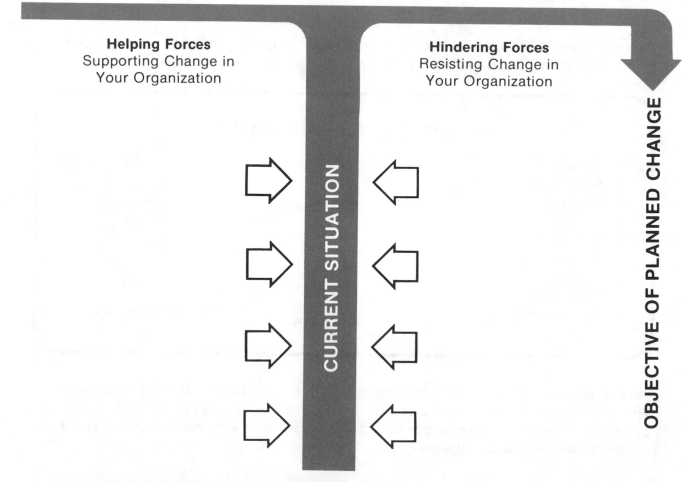

Helping Forces
Supporting Change in
Your Organization

Hindering Forces
Resisting Change in
Your Organization

CURRENT SITUATION

OBJECTIVE OF PLANNED CHANGE

*Adapted from John E. Jones and J. William Pfeiffer (Eds.), *The 1973 Annual Handbook for Group Facilitators.* La Jolla, Calif.: University Associates, 1973. Used with permission.

Now that you have listed helping and hindering forces, write a one-paragraph summary of how you think people in your organization will react to your plan. Indicate what problems you anticipate in getting your plan accepted and where these are most likely come from.

SUMMARIZE HOW YOU THINK PEOPLE IN YOUR ORGANIZATION WILL RESPOND TO YOUR PLAN

1. **Co-workers**

2. **Other staff**

3. **Managers**

4. **Policy makers**

EPILOGUE
D

Prepare your strategy for getting your plan accepted in your organization.

Strategies for Acceptance

Most of us know what it's like to come up with a beautiful idea for improving things—to write a brilliantly clear proposal and then find the idea rebuffed or, worse, simply ignored. That kind of thing doesn't happen too often before we stop trying to make things better and settle into apathy or indifference. But it's just not enough to have a wonderful idea or some great evaluative information about what change is needed, unless that idea can be put into practice or that feedback can be used in making decisions. To be effective, planners must be salespeople too!

So—now you have this well-thought-out plan. You've diligently followed Steps 1 through 6. You understand your own beliefs and attitudes about change, how receptive your organization is to change, how the change process typically occurs, and what problems you may encounter. Now comes the real question: "How am I going to get the right people to implement the plan?"

"...use the momentum and weight of your opponents to defeat them – leaving them unhurt, but where you want them!"

There are an infinite number of ways to gain acceptance for your plan. Here are some possible strategies and "words to the wise" to inspire your strategic thinking.

Use Judo*

One way to think about gaining acceptance of your plan is to think of the person or group you have to convince as if they were your opponents in the Japanese martial art of judo. In judo, being a short, light-weight person can be an advantage, because you can use the momentum and weight of your opponents to defeat them—leaving them unhurt, but where you want them.

In applying this approach to organizational change, the key point is to know the person(s) you are trying to convince and make it obvious to them how your plan is in line with their principles, values, or pet ideas. Despite the logic and rationality of Steps 1 through 6, we all know that decisions often are made more for emotional or ideological reasons than for "rational" reasons. The trick is to identify where the decision makers are coming from and use these emotions and values to sell your highly rational and well-thought-out proposal.

*Adapted from *The Soft Revolution* by Neil Postman and Charles Weingartner. Copyright © 1971 by Neil Postman and Charles Weingartner and used by permission of the publisher, Delacorte Press.

EPILOGUE
D

Know Your Innovation*

In getting ready to propose an innovation, it is useful to think through in advance how easy or difficult it will be to get people to accept it. Know your innovation, and anticipate questions and concerns that management and staff will have. Use these questions to assess how difficult your sales job will be.

1. What is the cost of implementing this change (including costs in time, money, social status)?

2. What are the potential benefits, in both the short- and long-run, for the organization and individuals?

3. How will the innovation make life easier for people in the organization (by cutting red tape or simplifying paperwork)?

4. How much risk or uncertainty is involved?

5. Whom can you count on for support and opposition inside and outside the organization?

6. How easy is it to communicate what the change is all about?

7. How compatible is this plan with the goals, values, and structure of the organization?

8. How complex are the changes that are involved?

9. Where did this idea come from? (It will help if others are already doing it or if it was proposed by someone respected by people in the organization.)

10. Can the plan be tried out on a small scale first?

11. Can the plan be modified without losing effectiveness? (If it has to be done in a certain precise way, it will be harder for people to accept.)

*These questions were formulated by Jesse E. Gordon, Professor of Psychology and Social Work, University of Michigan.

Give Them the Facts*

When you are telling other people about your plan, either verbally or in writing, use some of the following techniques. Note which ones you have used in other situations and how well they worked for you.

1. ***Explain why***—Provide all the facts about the reason for changing. If there are risks, acknowledge them, but tell why the risks are worth taking. Show what you have done to minimize the risk.

2. ***Name the benefits that could result from the change***—Don't exaggerate, but list them objectively. Not to do so would be like a sales person not telling a customer what the product can do.

3. ***Seek questions and answer them***—This will stop rumors that inevitably arise during an organizational change.

4. ***Invite participation***—Ask for suggestions, because the people involved know the situation best. Changes work out most favorably when those concerned have a part in suggesting the change.

5. ***Avoid surprise***—This stirs unreasoning opposition more than any other factor, because those involved don't have time to think. Their emotions take over, and such emotions are most likely to be negative.

6. ***Acknowledge the rough spots***—In selling an organizational change, we tend to make it sound simple, presenting a clearcut chart and neat lines of responsibility. But even a minor change is rarely simple. Admit it, and tell how you plan to smooth the shift.

...more ⟹

*Adapted from *Managing Change: The Strategies of Making Change Work for You*, by John S. Morgan. Copyright© 1972 by McGraw-Hill, Inc. Used with permission of McGraw-Hill Book Company.

EPILOGUE
D

FACTS CONTINUED

7. ***Set standards***—Give a date when you want the change to be completed. Tell what you want it to accomplish. What are the penalties for failure? The rewards for success?

8. ***Contact informal leaders***—Let them know in particular detail what is going on.

9. ***Praise***—People in any new situation are anxious, and positive reinforcement helps.

10. ***Repeat***—To get across something complex you must tell the story over and over, using fresh examples and different approaches.

Know Your Organization*

Your strategy for introducing an innovation will depend partly on whether your organization is open to change and encourages innovative ideas or whether it resists change and discourages new ideas. If you live in an innovation-resisting organization, your only alternatives may be tactics such as concealing the change from other parts of the organization, concealing the change from your supervisor, bringing in a "respectable" outsider as a consultant, or using a time of crisis to bring about change because everyone is desperate.

In an innovation-encouraging organization, the tactics are different. You can be open about what you propose and depend on others in the organization to give constructive criticism and share responsibility for implementation. It may be possible to build in processes of change—for example, an annual time for organizational self-evaluation and reflection. You may want to encourage openness and diversity of opinion in the planning and evaluation stages and allow the efficiency of a bureaucratic style to take over for the implementation stage.

*Adapted from Herbert Shepard, "Innovation-Resisting and Innovation-Producing Organizations," *Journal of Business*, Vol. 40, No. 4, October 1967. Copyright © 1967 by The University of Chicago. Used with permission of the University of Chicago Press.

EPILOGUE

D

Now, based on your knowledge of your plan and your organization and some of the techniques discussed above, what is your strategy for getting your plan accepted?

STRATEGY FOR IMPLEMENTATION

1. **WHO needs to be involved?**

2. **WHAT will they need to do? WHAT initial steps must be taken?**

3. **WHEN will each activity be done?**

4. **WHERE will this take place** (levels of the organization or places in the community)?

5. **HOW will you do it?**

Strategies for Acceptance

Monitor your progress as you carry out this implementation strategy. Be prepared to modify your initial approach if necessary.

EVALUATION OF IMPLEMENTATION STRATEGY

1. **Was your plan accepted?**

2. **What problems did you run into?**

3. **How did you modify your strategy?**

4. **What techniques were most effective for you?**

THE END

Planning can be frustrating—when people just don't cooperate or when your beautiful plan just doesn't work. But planning can also be fun—when you can pat yourself on the back as you check off an activity completed on schedule and when you find things moving along smoothly because you've thought everything out in advance.

Whenever you're faced with a problem in your organization, in your community, in your own work situation, or even in your home life, you'll be able to pull out the techniques you've learned from your **Hip Pocket Guide** and go to it. Good luck!

Planning &

Evaluation
Checklist

Before you implement your plan, you need to be sure you've covered all the bases. Review your plan, and check to be sure you've included these key elements.

GENERAL CONSIDERATIONS

HAVE YOU:

_____Been explicit about what you are trying to do, why you are doing it this way, and how you'll know how well you have done?

_____Involved key people in the planning and evaluation process?

STEP 1: DEFINING THE PROBLEM

DID YOU:

_____Discover as much as possible about the problem?

_____Define the problem clearly?

_____Write the problem statement to include the following basic points—future point in time you're concerned about, part of the organization that is involved, the nature of the problem, the size of the problem, and who the problem affects?

STEP 2: SETTING THE OBJECTIVE

DID YOU:

_____Describe the objective as a situation that you hope will exist in the future?

_____Indicate how you'll know when the desired situation exists?

STEP 3:
CHOOSING AMONG
ALTERNATE STRATEGIES

HAVE YOU:

_____Thought of as many alternatives as possible before deciding on which strategy you will follow?

_____Analyzed the feasibility of each strategy?

_____Involved other staff in choosing a strategy?

_____Been clear about why you chose the strategy that you did?

STEP 4:
PREPARING FOR
IMPLEMENTATION

DID YOU:

_____Figure out what major activities will be needed to carry out the strategy?

_____Set deadlines for when each major activity is to be completed?

_____Make a "public" chart showing deadlines and who is responsible?

_____Prepare a budget showing resources that will be needed?

STEP 5:
DESIGNING THE
EVALUATION

DID YOU:

_____Determine what decisions need to be made and what information is required before deciding what data to collect?

_____Design measures that will reveal how well you did in carrying out your plan and reaching your objective?

STEP 6:
USING EVALUATIVE
INFORMATION

ARE YOU CONVINCED THAT:

_____Feedback must be given in a way that increases the chances of its being accepted?

_____You need to provide the right people with the right information at the right time?

EPILOGUE:
INITIATING
ORGANIZATIONAL CHANGE

DO YOU KNOW:

_____How organizations change?

_____What problems you're likely to face in introducing your plan?

_____How you're going to go about getting your plan accepted?

Suggestions for Further Readings

HIP POCKET GUIDE
TO PLANNING & EVALUATION

SETTING THE OBJECTIVE

Mager, R. F. *Preparing instructional objectives*. Belmont, California: Fearon Publishers, 1972.

CHOOSING AMONG ALTERNATE STRATEGIES

Hall, J. Decisions, decisions, decisions. *Psychology Today*, November 1971, pp. 51–54.

Jones, J. E., & Pfeiffer, J. W. (Eds.). *The 1973 annual handbook for group facilitators*. La Jolla, California: University Associates, 1973.

Pfeiffer, J. W., & Jones, J. E. (Eds.). *A handbook of structured experiences for human relations training* (Vol. 2). La Jolla, California: University Associates Publishers, 1974.

PREPARING FOR IMPLEMENTATION

Morris, R., & Binstock, R. *Feasible planning for social change*. New York: Columbia University Press, 1965.

DESIGNING THE EVALUATION

Deniston, O. L. *Evaluation of disease control programs*. Washington, D.C.: U.S. Public Health Service, 1972.

Tripodi, T., Fellin, P., & Epstein, I. *Social program evaluation: Guidelines for health, education and welfare administrators*. Ithaca, New York: F. E. Peacock, 1971.

Weiss, C. H. *Evaluation research: Methods for assessing program effectiveness*. Englewood Cliffs, New Jersey: Prentice-Hall, 1972.

INITIATING ORGANIZATIONAL CHANGE

Beckhard, R. *Organization development: Strategies and models*. Reading, Mass.: Addison-Wesley Publishing Co., 1969.

Bennis, W., Benne, K. D., & Chin, R. (Eds.). *The planning of change* (2nd ed.). New York: Holt, Rinehart and Winston, 1969. (Especially articles by Robert Chin and Kenneth Benne: "General Strategies for Effecting Changes in Human Systems," and by Herbert Shepard: "Innovation-Resisting and Innovation-Producing Organization")

Cooper, J. D. *The art of decision-making.* Garden City, New York: Doubleday & Co., 1961.

Greiner, L. E. Patterns of organizational change. *Harvard Business Review,* 1967, *45* (3), 119–122.

Lewin, K. Frontiers in group dynamics: Concepts, method and reality in social science; Social equilibria and social change. *Human Relations,* 1947, *1* (1), 5–41.

Likert, R. *The human organization: Its management and value.* New York: McGraw-Hill Book Co., 1967.

Lippitt, R., Watson, J., & Westley, B. *The dynamics of planned change—A comparative study of principles and techniques.* New York: Harcourt, Brace & World, 1958.

Morgan, J. S. *Managing change; The strategies of making change work for you.* New York: McGraw-Hill Book Co., 1972.

Postman, N., & Weingartner, C. *The soft revolution: A student handbook for turning schools around.* New York: Dell Publishing Co., 1971.

Reddin, W. J. *Managerial effectiveness.* New York: McGraw-Hill Book Co., 1970.

Schein, E. H. *Process consultation: Its role in organization development.* Reading, Mass.: Addison-Wesley Publishing Co., 1969.

Shepard, H. Innovation-resisting and innovation-producing organizations. *Journal of Business,* 1967, *40* (4), 470–477.

OVERALL FORMAT

Deniston, O. L. *Program planning for disease control programs* (Rev. ed.). Washington, D.C.: U. S. Public Health Service, 1972.

Kobert, D., & Bagnall, J *The universal traveler: A companion for those on problem-solving journeys and a soft-systems guidebook to the process of design.* Los Altos, California: William Kaufmann, 1973.

ABOUT THE AUTHOR

In preparing the **Hip Pocket Guide** and **Trainer's Handbook,** Dorothy P. Craig has drawn from her wide-ranging experience in social service, program development, community planning, and public administration.

She originally created the **Guide** for use in a staff development and continuing education project to improve the organizational effectiveness of mental health agencies in the Detroit area. The practical foundations for the book were laid during four years as a planner and administrator with the Macomb County (Michigan) Community Mental Health Services, at a time of rapid agency expansion.

Dorothy has a bachelor's degree from Allegheny College—where she was editor-in-chief of the newspaper—and a master's degree in social work policy and administration from the University of Michigan. She has also taken part in numerous workshops on organizational development and personal growth.

Now a resident of the Pacific Northwest, Dorothy worked for three years for the King County (Washington) Planning Division. She assisted several small towns in the Snoqualmie Valley with community planning, and most recently was contracts manager for the county's five-million-dollar housing and community development program.

At present, Dorothy is editing manuscripts and developing training materials on a freelance basis. Her personal goals include building her own solar-heated home on the Olympic Peninsula, raising vegetables, and creating a self-sufficient lifestyle.